P9-CEI-601

Better Homes and Gardens®
Great Patchwork
Collection
A Step-by-Step Guide to Quilting

Better Homes and Gardens®
Des Moines, Iowa

Better Homes and Gardens® Books
An imprint of Meredith® Books

Better Homes and Gardens® Great Patchwork Collection
Editor: Carol Field Dahlstrom
Contributing Technical Editor: Susan Banker
Contributing Graphic Designer: Gayle Schadendorf
Copy Chief: Angela K. Renkoski
Photographer: Steven Mays
Electronic Production Coordinator: Paula Forest
Production Manager: Douglas Johnston
Prepress Coordinator: Marjorie J. Schenkelberg

Meredith® Books
Editor in Chief: James D. Blume
Managing Editor: Christopher Cavanaugh
Director, New Product Development: Ray Wolf
Vice President, General Manager: Jamie L. Martin

Better Homes and Gardens® Magazine
Editor in Chief: Jean LemMon

Meredith Publishing Group
President, Publishing Group: Christopher Little
Vice President and Publishing Director: John Loughlin

Meredith Corporation
Chairman of the Board and Chief Executive Officer: Jack D. Rehm
President and Chief Operating Officer: William T. Kerr
Chairman of the Executive Committee: E.T. Meredith III

Cover Photograph: Wm. Hopkins, Hopkins Associates
On the cover: Striped Sashing Quilt, see page 7.

All of us at Better Homes and Gardens Books are dedicated to providing you with the information and ideas you need to create beautiful quilts. We welcome your questions, comments, or suggestions. Please write to us at: Better Homes and Gardens Books, Crafts Editorial Department, RW 240, 1716 Locust Street, Des Moines, IA 50309-3023.

© Copyright 1997 by Meredith Corporation, Des Moines, Iowa.
All rights reserved. Printed in the United States of America.
First Edition. Printing Number and Year: 5 4 3 2 1 01 00 99 98 97
Library of Congress Catalog Card Number: 96-78796
ISBN: 0-696-20645-5

*W*hether we find ourselves snuggling
under our favorite patchwork quilt or admiring
Grandmother's quilted stitches displayed in a position of
prominence, quilts add pleasure, pride, and personal
warmth to our lives. Pieced from vintage scraps or
stitched with exciting new fabrics, quilts are crafted
works of art to enjoy.

Now you can create an heirloom quilt
of your very own with our collection of traditional
patterns and our step-by-step instructions. Every part
of the quiltmaking process is explained in detail with
illustrations to make your quilting experience
rewarding and successful.

We're sure you'll enjoy this most
exceptional collection of great patchwork designs
as you create very special quilts that will
deserve generations of love.

Table of Contents

Successful Quilting

To assure your success and satisfaction we've designed this book
with every step you'll need to stitch an heirloom quilt. First we'll
take a look at the components to give you an idea of how the quilt
goes together. Then, you'll learn how to cut the pieces, adjust the
size, and assemble and finish your quilting project.

Throughout construction, you can rely on our diagrams and
instructions to be helpful and precise. Plus we'll share tips on
everything from how to save fabric to the best piecing ideas and
accessory options. And should you have any questions, we have
included a quilting basics section on pages 197-239. These pages
contain invaluable quilting information you'll refer to time and
time again.

Part of the fun of quilting is choosing your fabrics, colors, and
prints. We'll show you alternatives to the fabrics we have selected
for each project and invite you to use your imagination. Before
long, you'll feel confident experimenting with color schemes and
may even want to try quilting a design of your own!

With all the secrets of successful quilting revealed and with all
these quilter-tested designs to choose from, it's time to create
your very own keepsake quilt!

Striped Sashing Quilt

This quilt is about one hundred years old and the pattern
was most likely created by its maker. The simple trellis design of stripes
and diamonds has an almost whirligig energy. The allover quilting pattern is
just a diamond grid, but the plain blocks could be filled with any quilting pattern.
If you would like a more challenging project, think of setting this sashing
around pieced blocks. The striped portion of the sashing can be
strip-pieced or cut from striped fabric.

Note: All dimensions except for binding are finished size.
Amounts for full/queen are given in parentheses.

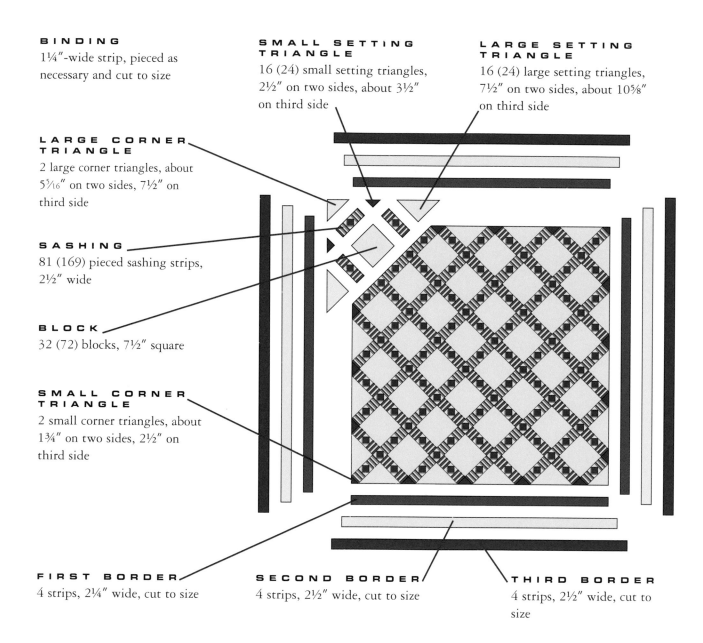

BINDING
1¼"-wide strip, pieced as necessary and cut to size

LARGE CORNER TRIANGLE
2 large corner triangles, about 5⁵⁄₁₆" on two sides, 7½" on third side

SASHING
81 (169) pieced sashing strips, 2½" wide

BLOCK
32 (72) blocks, 7½" square

SMALL CORNER TRIANGLE
2 small corner triangles, about 1¾" on two sides, 2½" on third side

SMALL SETTING TRIANGLE
16 (24) small setting triangles, 2½" on two sides, about 3½" on third side

LARGE SETTING TRIANGLE
16 (24) large setting triangles, 7½" on two sides, about 10⅝" on third side

FIRST BORDER
4 strips, 2¼" wide, cut to size

SECOND BORDER
4 strips, 2½" wide, cut to size

THIRD BORDER
4 strips, 2½" wide, cut to size

FABRIC AND CUTTING LIST

Note: Sizes and amounts for full/queen are given in parentheses.

Yardages are based on 44"-wide fabric. Prepare templates, if desired, referring to drafting schematics. Cut strips and patches following schematics and chart. Cut binding as directed below. Except for drafting schematics, which give finished sizes, all dimensions include ¼" seam allowance and strips include extra length, unless otherwise stated. (Note: Angles on all patches are either 45° or 90°.)

DIMENSIONS

FINISHED BLOCK
7½" square; about 10⅝" diagonal

FINISHED QUILT
About 78" (106¼") square

MATERIALS

MUSLIN SOLID
5½ (7¼) yds.

RED SOLID
2½ (3¼) yds.

NAVY PRINT
2½ (3¼) yds.

BINDING
½ yd. lt. blue solid, cut and pieced to make a 1¼" × 340" (1¼" × 460") strip.

BACKING *
5¼ (10) yds.

BATTING *

THREAD

*Backing and batting should be cut and pieced as necessary so they are at least 4" larger than quilt top on all sides, then trimmed to size after quilting.

DRAFTING SCHEMATICS
(No seam allowance added)

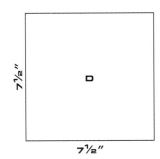

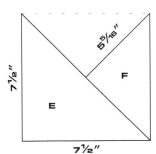

GREAT TIME-SAVING TIPS

You can use a single fabric with ½"-wide stripes (1¾ yds. for twin, 2¼ yds. for full/queen) instead of strip-piecing two different fabrics for each striped sashing unit. Cut each unit 3" square.

9

FIRST CUT			SECOND CUT	
Fabric and Yardage	Number of Pieces	Size	Number of Pieces	Shape
PLAIN PATCHES				
Muslin Solid 3 (4) yds.	6	2⅛″ × 81″ (2⅛″ × 108″)	452 (596)	A[1]
	7 (15)	8″ × 40″	32 (72)	D
	4 (5)	5¹⁵⁄₁₆″ × 40″	16 (24)	E
	1	4⅜″ × 20″	2	F
Red Solid[2]	3	2¼″ × 90″ (2¼″ × 117″)	113 (149)	B
	1	2⅛″ × 50″ (2⅛″ × 70″)	16 (24)	G
	1	1⅞″ × 10″	2	H
FIRST BORDER[3]				
Navy Print 2½ (3¼) yds.	2	2¾″ × 72″ (2¾″ × 100″)		
	2	2¾″ × 76″ (2¾″ × 104″)		
SECOND BORDER[3]				
Muslin Solid 2½ (3¼) yds.	2	3″ × 76″ (3″ × 104″)		
	2	3″ × 81″ (3″ × 109″)		
THIRD BORDER[3]				
Red Solid 2½ (3¼) yds.	2	3″ × 81″ (3″ × 109″)		
	2	3″ × 86″ (3″ × 114″)		

[1] Cut A's from remainder of fabric from second border.
[2] Cut B's, G's and H's from remainder of fabric from third border.
[3] Reserve remainder of fabric for cutting patches.

FIRST CUT			SECOND CUT		
Fabric and Yardage	Number of Pieces	Size	Method	Number of Pieces	Shape
STRIP-PIECED PATCHES[1]					
Navy Print and Muslin Solid	18 (30)	1″ × 81″ (1″ × 108″)	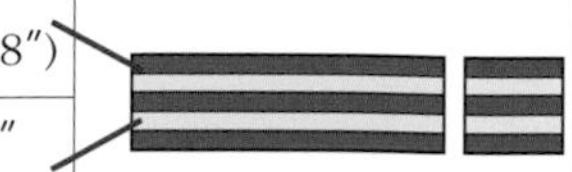 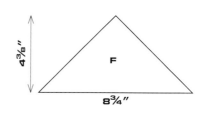	162 (338)	C/C/C/C/C 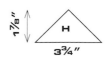
	12 (20)	1″ × 81″ (1″ × 108″)			

[1] Cut strips from remainder of fabric from first and second borders; see also the *Great Time-Saving Tips*, page 9. Join strips lengthwise, alternating colors as shown.

CUTTING SCHEMATICS
(Seam allowance included)

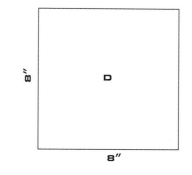

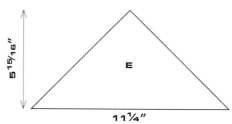

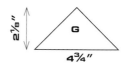

The size of this quilt can be adjusted easily from twin to full/queen if the number of components is increased to make four additional rows of blocks and four additional rows of sashing.

TWIN

32 blocks, quilt center about 63½" square

FULL/QUEEN

72 blocks, quilt center about 91¾" square

QUILT ASSEMBLY

Sashing

Directions are given below for twin. Differing amounts for full/queen are given in parentheses.

1. Join 4 A's to a B to make a square-in-a-square. Make 113 (149).

2. Join 2 C/C/C/C/C squares to a square-in-a-square to make a sashing strip. Make 81 (169).

Quilt Center

Arrange units as shown. Join units to make rows.
Join rows.

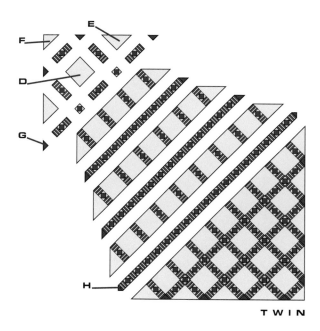

T W I N

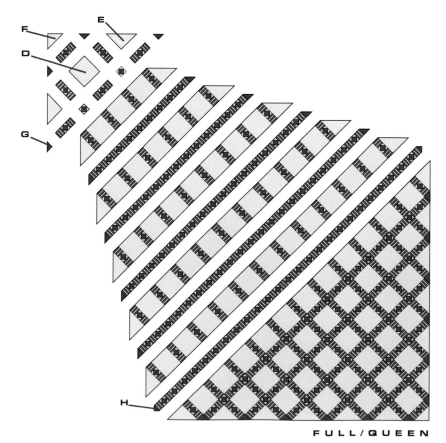

F U L L / Q U E E N

Borders

Join borders to quilt center, first shorter strips at top
and bottom, then longer strips at sides. Complete first border
before proceeding to second, then third.

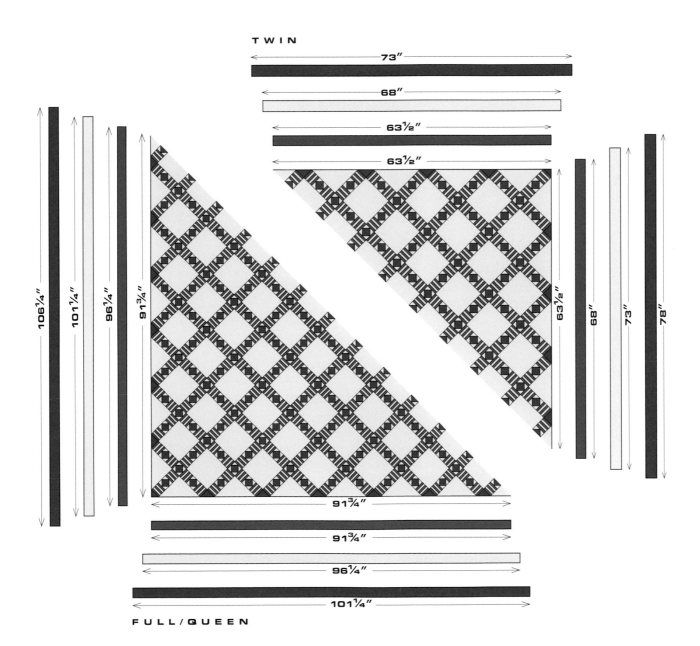

Finishing

The quilting design used in this antique is a simple diagonal grid. The diamonds on one diagonal half of the quilt are perpendicular to those on the other half.

1. Divide quilt diagonally along the line indicated by the arrow in the second illustration. Mark quilting design on quilt top. Do not mark seams.

◆ *For quilt center:* Mark vertical lines 1″ apart on D's and E's on first half of quilt, using corners of C's as a guide. Mark horizontal lines on second half of quilt in same manner.

◆ *For quilt center and borders:* Mark 45° diagonal lines in opposite directions on each half of quilt. Draw lines 1″ apart and parallel to block edges.

2. Prepare batting and backing.

3. Assemble quilt layers.

4. Quilt on all marked lines and in-the-ditch on sashing seams to make diagonal lines continuous on each half of quilt.

5. Trim batting and backing to 1¼″ beyond outermost seam line.

6. Bind quilt edges.

The way you place color in this pattern will change its appearance as much
as the palette you use. Note how different it looks when you make the plain blocks
the same color as the small squares. If you make the perpendicular bands of
sashing from contrasting colors, you will create a plaid.

Photocopy this page, then create your own color scheme using colored pencils or markers. Refer to the examples shown, or design a unique arrangement to match your decor or please your fancy. Experiment to see what happens when you make alternate or adjacent plain blocks from different colors.

Starry Path Pillow

*H*ere the traditional Starry Path block is paired with an original clipper ship design, which was pieced to accompany the multicolored star and simply quilted to finish the red one. Note the illusion of intertwined triangles which emerges when each point of the star is a different color.

Note: All dimensions are finished size.

STARRY PATH BLOCK
One block, 10″ square

BOAT BLOCK
4 blocks, 2″ square

FIRST BORDER
4 pieced strips, 2″ wide, cut to size

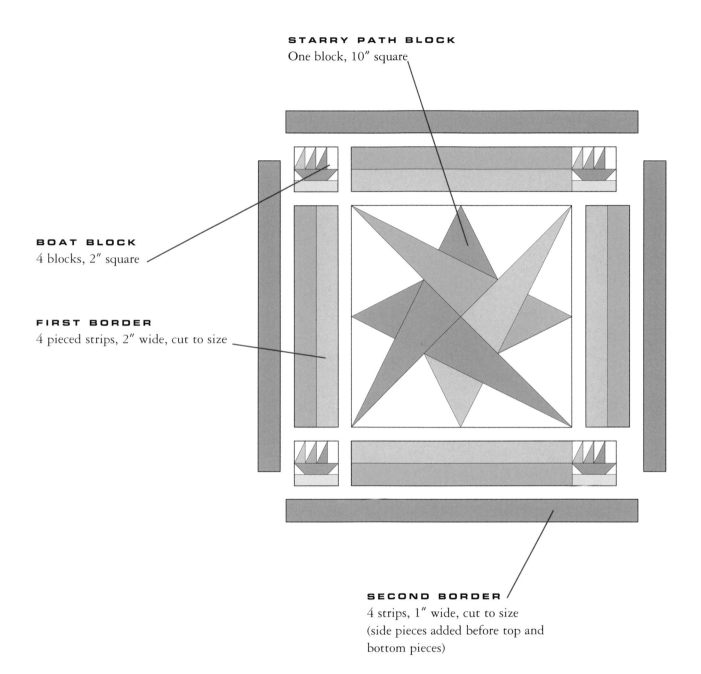

SECOND BORDER
4 strips, 1″ wide, cut to size
(side pieces added before top and
bottom pieces)

*Note: To make the red-and-blue variation, see the **Great Ideas** on page 23.*

Yardages are based on 44″-wide fabric. Prepare templates for Starry Path block, referring to drafting schematic, below, or actual-size patterns on page 25; prepare templates for Boat block, if desired, using actual-size block pattern, below. Cut strips and patches following chart. Except for drafting schematic, which gives finished sizes, all dimensions include ¼″ seam allowance and strips include extra length, unless otherwise stated.

DIMENSIONS

FINISHED STARRY PATH BLOCK
10″ square, about 14⅛″ diagonal

FINISHED BOAT BLOCK
2″ square, about 2⅞″ diagonal

FINISHED PILLOW
16″ square

MATERIALS

- **RED PRINT**
  ¼ yd.
- **BLUE PRINT**
  ¼ yd.
- **OLIVE PRINT**
  ¼ yd.
- **WHITE PRINT**
  ½ yd.
- **BLUE FLORAL**
  ¼ yd.
- **BLUE SOLID**
  ¼ yd.
- **BACKING** *
  ½ yd.
- **PILLOW BACK**
  ½ yd.
- **BATTING** *
- **FIBERFILL FOR STUFFING**
- **THREAD**

*Backing and batting should be cut and pieced as necessary so they are at least 4″ larger than quilt top on all sides, then trimmed to size after quilting.

DRAFTING SCHEMATIC
(No seam allowance added)

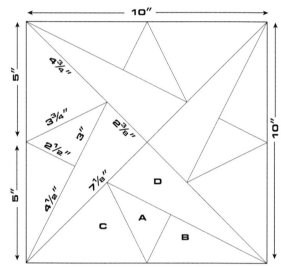

STARRY PATH BLOCK

ACTUAL-SIZE PATTERN
(No seam allowance added)

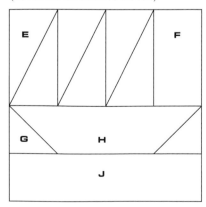

BOAT BLOCK

| Fabric and Yardage | FIRST CUT | | SECOND CUT | | |
| | Number of Pieces | Size | Number of Pieces | | Shape |
			For One Starry Path Block	For 4 Boat Blocks	
PLAIN PATCHES					
Blue Floral[1]	–	–	1	–	A 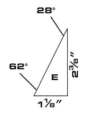
	–	–	1	–	D
	1	1⅛″ × 5″	–	4	E
Blue Print[1]	–	–	1	–	A
	–	–	1	–	D
	1	1⅛″ × 5″	–	4	E
Olive Print[1]	–	–	1	–	A
	–	–	1	–	D
	1	1⅛″ × 5″	–	4	E
Red Print ¼ yd.	–	–	1	–	A
	–	–	1	–	D
	1	1″ × 16″	–	4	H
Blue Solid ¼ yd.	1	1″ × 16″	–	4	J
White Print ½ yd.	1	3⅜″ × 15″	4	–	B
	1	4¼″ × 25″	4	–	C
	1	1⅞″ × 20″	–	12	E
	1	1½″ × 8″	–	4	F
	1	1⅜″ × 8″	–	8	G

[1] Use remainder of fabric from border strips.

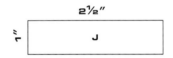

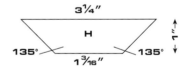

| Fabric and Yardage | FIRST CUT | | SECOND CUT | |
	Number of Pieces	Size	Number of Pieces	Size
FIRST BORDER				
Olive Print[1] ¼ yd.	2	1½″ × 24″	4	1½″ × 12″
Blue Print[1] ¼ yd.	2	1½″ × 24″	4	1½″ × 12″
SECOND BORDER				
Blue Floral[1] ¼ yd.	1	1½″ × 32″	2	1½″ × 16″
	1	1½″ × 36″	2	1½″ × 18″

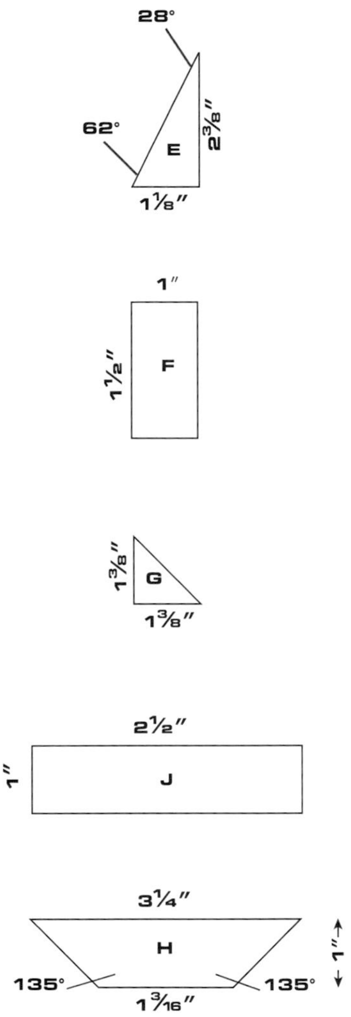

[1] Reserve remainder of fabric for plain patches.

Starry Path Block

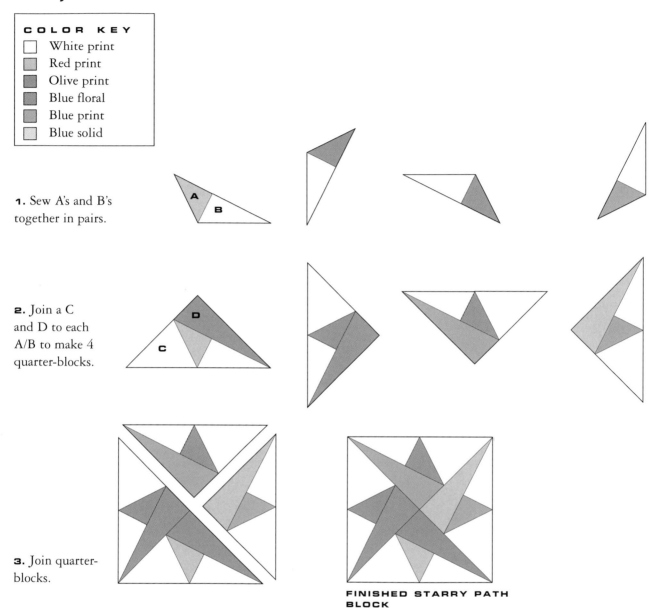

COLOR KEY
- ☐ White print
- ☐ Red print
- ☐ Olive print
- ☐ Blue floral
- ☐ Blue print
- ☐ Blue solid

1. Sew A's and B's together in pairs.

2. Join a C and D to each A/B to make 4 quarter-blocks.

3. Join quarter-blocks.

FINISHED STARRY PATH BLOCK

Boat Block

Directions are given below for making one block. Amounts for making all 4 blocks at the same time are in parentheses.

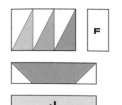
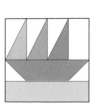

1. Join E's in pairs to make 3 (12) sail rectangles. Join rectangles.

2. Sew G's to H to make one (4) boat bottom.

3. Arrange pieced and plain units in rows as shown. Join rows.

FINISHED BOAT BLOCK

22

Borders

1. Join strips for first border in pairs. Trim pieced strips to same length as sides of Starry Path block.

2. Sew Boat blocks to ends of 2 pieced strips.

3. Join borders to Starry Path block, short strips at sides and then longer strips at top and bottom.

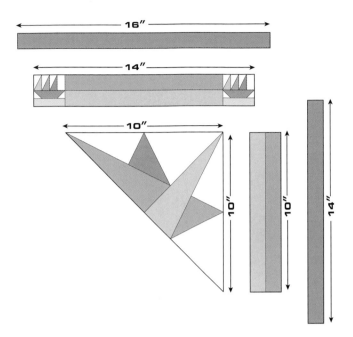

Finishing

1. Prepare batting and backing.
2. Assemble layers for quilting.
3. Quilt in-the-ditch on all seams.
4. Trim batting and backing even with pillow front. Cut pillow back same size.
5. Stitch pillow front and back together, leaving an opening in one side for turning and stuffing. Turn pillow right side out.
6. Stuff pillow. Slipstitch opening closed.

GREAT IDEAS

You can give the Starry Path block a bold new look just by changing the colors. To make the red-and-blue variation, cut all As, Ds, and the second border from red print fabric. Cut all Bs and Cs from blue print. Cut strips for the first border from white print and blue floral.

To make super-easy Boat blocks, cut four 2½" squares from white print fabric (seam allowance included) and quilt the boats instead of piecing them, using the actual-size pattern on page 20.

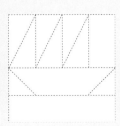

These pillows look very different as the number of colors increases or the background shifts from dark to light. They're good scrap projects, so check the contents of your stash, considering how the scale of different prints will alter the design.

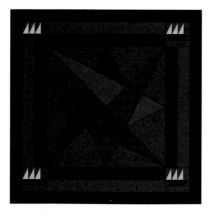

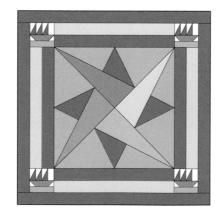

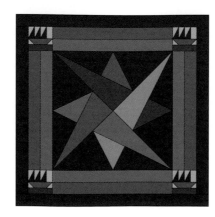

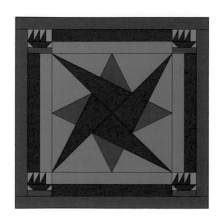

Starry Path Pillow

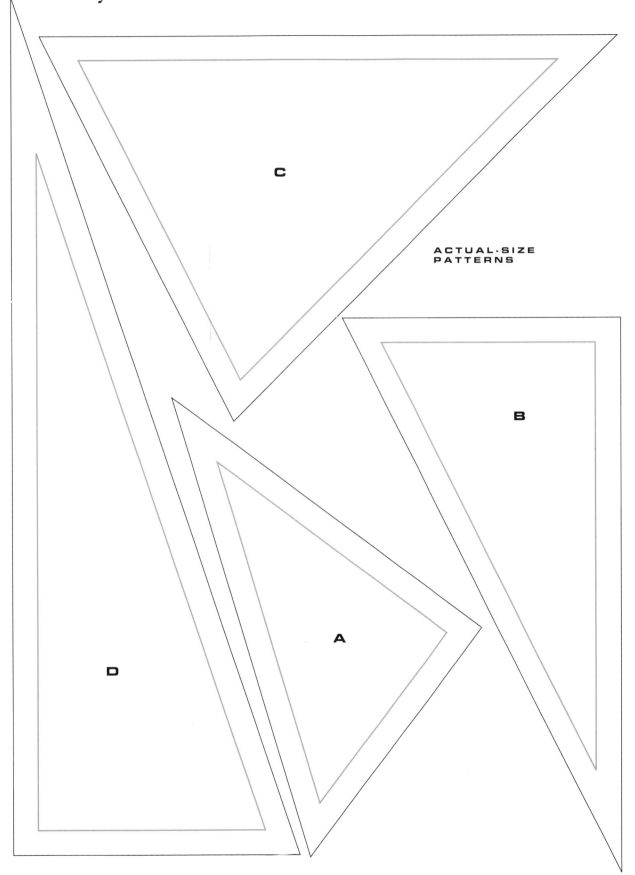

C

ACTUAL-SIZE
PATTERNS

B

A

D

Broken Dishes

*T*he maker of this wonderful nineteenth century doll quilt chose
delicate prints for her bold patchwork. The tiny flounce scrolling across the plum
fabric is echoed by the ruffled edging, and wispy green flowers dot the ecru patches
while a beautiful green-on-ecru paisley covers the back. The quiltmaker omitted
batting and the quilt is very soft and light. Easy triangle-triangle squares
make short work of the piecing, making it an excellent project to do
with a young quilter.

Note: All dimensions except for ruffle are finished size.

BLOCK
16 blocks, 3¾″ square

SHORT SASHING STRIP
12 strips, 1½″ × 3¾″

LONG SASHING STRIP
5 strips, 1½″ × 19½″

RUFFLE
2½″-wide strip, pieced as necessary and cut to size

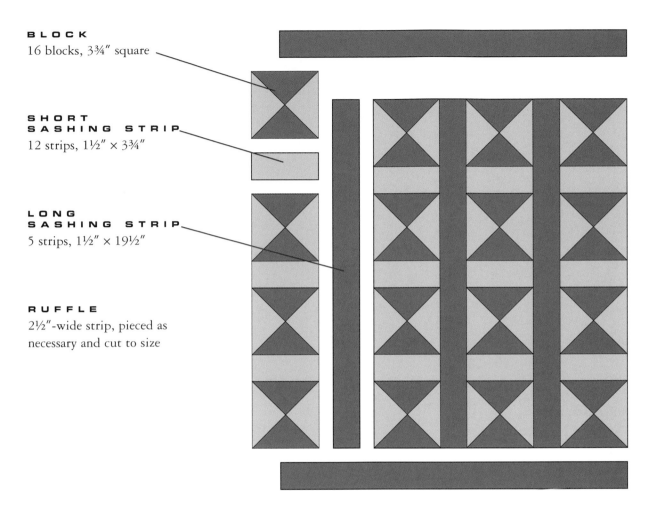

GREAT SIZING TIPS

Because this pattern will repeat continuously no matter how many blocks are placed in each row or column, you can plan your quilt to be almost any size you wish. Just remember that the length of each edge will be a multiple of 3¾″ (one block) plus a multiple of 1½″ (the width of each sashing strip). Some examples:

4 blocks in a 2 x 2 layout with sashing = 9″ x 12″ hotpad

24 blocks in a 3 x 8 layout with sashing = 14¼″ x 43½″ table runner

70 blocks in a 7 x 10 layout with sashing = 35¼″ x 54″ crib quilt

Y̲ardages are based on 44"-wide fabric. Prepare templates, if desired, referring to drafting schematics. Cut strips and patches following cutting schematics and chart. Cut ruffle as directed below. Except for drafting schematics, which give finished sizes, all dimensions include ¼" seam allowance and strips include extra length, unless otherwise stated.
(Note: Angles on all patches are either 45° or 90°.)

DIMENSIONS

FINISHED BLOCK
3¾" square; about 5½" diagonal

FINISHED QUILT
19½" × 22½"

MATERIALS

ECRU/GREEN PRINT
¼ yd.

PLUM PRINT
¾ yd.

RUFFLE
Use ½ yd. plum print, cut and pieced, to make a 2½" × 200" straight-grain strip. Reserve remainder of fabric for cutting triangle-triangle squares.

BACKING *
¾ yd.

BATTING *

THREAD

*Backing and batting should be cut and pieced as necessary so they are at least 4" larger than quilt on all sides, then trimmed to size after quilting.

FIRST CUT			SECOND CUT	
Fabric and Yardage	Number of Pieces	Size	Number of Pieces	Shape
PLAIN PATCHES				
Ecru/Green Print[1] ¼ yd.	2	2" × 30"	12	A
Plum Print ¼ yd.	5	2" × 20" (exact length)		
SPEEDY TRIANGLE-TRIANGLE SQUARES[2]				
Ecru/Green Print[3]	4	6" × 11"	16	B/B/B/B
Plum Print[4]	4	6" × 11"		

[1] Reserve remainder of fabric for cutting triangle-triangle squares.
[2] See *Speedy Triangle-Triangle Squares*, page 221. Mark 1 × 2 grids of 5" squares.
[3] Use remainder of fabric from plain patches.
[4] Use remainder of fabric from ruffle.

DRAFTING SCHEMATICS
(No seam allowance added)

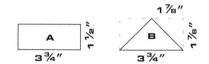

CUTTING SCHEMATICS
(Seam allowance included)

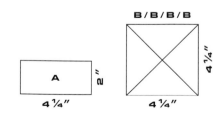

Quilt Center

B / B / B / B

A

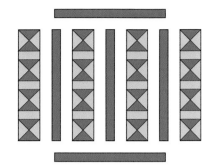

1. Join 4 triangle-triangle squares and 3 short sashing strips to make a column. Make 4.

2. Arrange units as shown. First join columns and long vertical sashing strips, then join long horizontal sashing strips at quilt top and bottom.

Finishing

1. Make ruffle and join it to quilt top; see *Ruffles*, page 234. Ruffle should face inward; do not press it away from quilt until after edges have been bound.

2. Prepare batting and backing.

3. Assemble quilt layers.

4. Quilt if desired, but no closer than ½″ to outermost seam line; see the *Great Quilting Ideas,* below.

5. Bind quilt edges.

◆ Trim batting even with outermost seam line on quilt top. Trim backing even with quilt top.

◆ Press under ¼″ at edges of quilt top and backing, align folds, and slipstitch together.

◆ Press ruffle away from quilt center.

6. Single-outline quilt ⅛″ inside the perimeter of the quilt.

GREAT QUILTING IDEAS

The stitcher of this project quilted it only at the outer edge, but you can add internal quilting as well, if you prefer. Some examples:

◆ Quilt in-the-ditch on all seams.
◆ Outline- or echo-quilt the blocks.
◆ Quilt motifs on the blocks and/or sashing.
◆ Quilt an allover geometric design.
◆ Stipple the sashing.

Just making the sashing and adjacent triangles in the same color will alter the overall appearance of this pattern. Or, try using a third color for all the sashing—and make each block different. Make each quadrant of the block from a different color, and the pattern will change again. Use colors with less contrast to soften the look.

If you omit the sashing and rotate alternate blocks one-quarter turn, you will really see the smashed china this pattern is named for. Place colors selectively to create all sorts of secondary overall patterns. Note that the blocks in these illustrations have all been set diagonally, with half-blocks completing the pattern.

Bull's-Eye

Simple and strong, Bull's-Eye is one of the easiest patchwork patterns. All the border strips are the same width, all the corner squares are the same size, and the piecing is a snap. This graphic pattern also offers a good opportunity for the color-shy to experiment with the palette. The mini quilt was stitched as a swatch to test the color combination and it was so charming that we couldn't resist finishing it with a prairie point border.

Note: All dimensions except for binding are finished size.

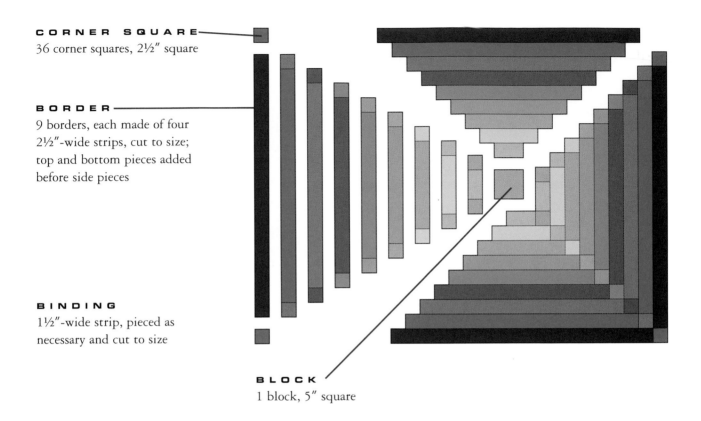

CORNER SQUARE

36 corner squares, 2½″ square

BORDER

9 borders, each made of four 2½″-wide strips, cut to size; top and bottom pieces added before side pieces

BINDING

1½″-wide strip, pieced as necessary and cut to size

BLOCK

1 block, 5″ square

GREAT SIZING TIPS

Because this pattern will repeat continuously no matter how many borders are placed around the quilt center, you can plan your quilt to be almost any size you wish; see the *Great Border Tips*, page 38, and the *Great Changing-the-Shape Tips*, page 39. Just remember that the length of each edge will be a multiple of 5″ (width of each center block; also the width of each pair of border strips). Some examples:

6 borders = 35″-square wallhanging
12 borders = 65″-square wallhanging
15 borders = 80″-square twin quilt

Yardages are based on 44″-wide fabric. Prepare templates, if desired, referring to drafting schematics. Cut strips and patches following cutting schematics and charts. Cut binding following cutting schematics, charts, and directions, below. Except for drafting schematics, which give finished sizes, all dimensions include ¼″ seam allowance. Except for overall binding length, all strips are exact length.
(Note: Angles on all patches are 90°.)

DIMENSIONS

FINISHED QUILT
50″ square

GREAT BINDING TIPS

If you want to make straight-grain binding from a single print, you will need an additional ½ yd. of fabric.

To make a single-print bias binding, you will need ¾ yd. of fabric. Cut strips on a 45° diagonal and piece as needed.

MATERIALS

LT. MUSTARD PRINT
½ yd.

MED. MUSTARD PRINT
¾ yd.

DK. MUSTARD PRINT
¾ yd.

LT. GREEN PLAID
¼ yd.

MED. GREEN PRINT
½ yd.

DK. GREEN PRINT
1¼ yds.

LT. LAVENDER PRINT
¼ yd.

MED. VIOLET PRINT
½ yd.

DK. RED-VIOLET PRINT
1½ yds.

BINDING
Use remainder of fabric from first, fourth, and seventh borders, cut and pieced, to make a 1½″ × 210½″ straight-grain strip; see schematics and cutting chart.

BACKING *
3½ yds.

BATTING *

THREAD

*Backing and batting should be cut and pieced as necessary so they are at least 4″ larger than quilt on all sides, then trimmed to size after quilting.

FIRST CUT			SECOND CUT	
Fabric and Yardage	Number of Pieces	Size	Number of Pieces	Size/Shape
PLAIN PATCHES[1]				
Lt. Mustard Print[2] ½ yd.	—	—	4	B
	1	3″ × 40″	4	3″ × 5½″
Med. Mustard Print[2] ¾ yd.	—	—	4	B
	4	3″ × 20½″		
Dk. Mustard Print[2] ¾ yd.	—	—	4	B
	4	3″ × 35½″		
Lt. Green Plaid ¼ yd.	—	—	4	B
	2	3″ × 40″	4	3″ × 10½″
Med. Green Print ½ yd.	—	—	4	B
	4	3″ × 25½″		
Dk. Green Print 1¼ yds.	—	—	4	B
	4	3″ × 40½″		
Lt. Lavender Print ¼ yd.	—	—	1	A
	—	—	8	B
	2	3″ × 40″	4	3″ × 15½″
Med. Violet Print ½ yd.	—	—	4	B
	4	3″ × 30½″		
Dk. Red-Violet Print 1½ yds.	4	3″ × 45½″		

[1]Cut strips first, then cut squares from remainder of fabric.
[2]Reserve remainder of fabric for binding.

DRAFTING SCHEMATICS
(No seam allowance added)

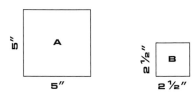

CUTTING SCHEMATICS
(Seam allowance included)

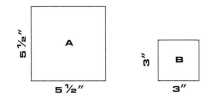

C / C / C

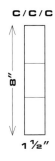

FIRST CUT			SECOND CUT		
Fabric and Yardage	Number of Pieces	Size	Method	Number of Pieces	Shape
STRIP-PIECED BINDING*					
Lt. Mustard Print, Med. Mustard Print, Dk. Mustard Print	2	3″ × 40″		28	C/C/C
	2	3″ × 40″			
	2	3″ × 40″			
*Use remainder of fabric from borders and plain patches. Join strips lengthwise as shown.					

GREAT DESIGN IDEAS

You can make a mini quilt by reducing the size of the components in the full-size wallhanging. Cut the center block 2″ square, and the border strips and corner squares 1¼″ wide.

Assemble the quilt top, then cut 24 light green squares, each 2⅝″ square, to make prairie point edging with 6 points on each side as shown below; see *Prairie Points*, page 233.

Borders

Join borders to quilt center in sequential order (all sides of first border, then second border, etc.) as directed below.

1. Stitch corner squares to side strips.

2. Join each border to quilt center, first plain strips at top and bottom, then pieced strips at sides.

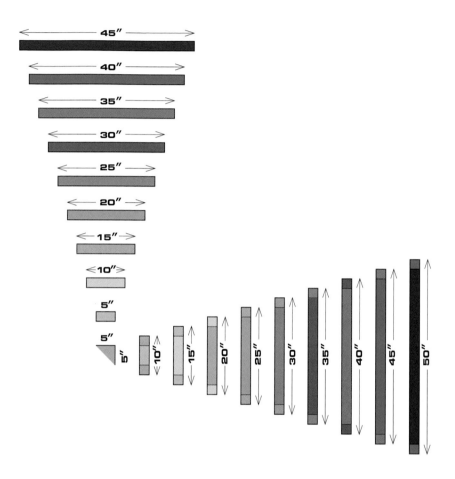

If you study the borders on the Bull's-Eye quilt, you will notice three distinct bands, each made of three consecutive borders. The bands generally progress in value from light to dark as your eye moves from the first band outward.

Each color (mustard, green, and purple) is used for one set of strips and one set of corner squares in each band, and the colors are in the same relative locations on all bands. Notice also that the color and value of the corner squares in each border are the same as those of the strips in the previous border, which results in light corner squares in the medium-value band and medium squares in the dark-value band.

To maintain the integrity of the pattern when changing the size of your quilt, increase or decrease the number of borders in groups of three (one complete band). If you are increasing the number of bands, plan your quilt so that the bands darken from the center outward; see also *Changing Colors* on page 40 for other arrangements.

Finishing

1. Mark quilting designs on quilt top.
- *For square patches:* Mark diagonal lines connecting pairs of opposite corners.
2. Prepare batting and backing.
3. Assemble quilt layers.
4. Quilt in-the-ditch on all seams. Quilt on all marked lines.

5. Trim batting and backing to ½″ beyond outermost seam line.
6. Prepare binding.
- *For three-print binding:* Join C/C/C units to make a 1½″ × 210½″ strip (extra length included).
7. Bind quilt edges.

GREAT CHANGING-THE-SHAPE TIPS

You can design a rectangular version of the Bull's-Eye quilt by changing the shape of the quilt center. Add one or more blocks to the center to make a row, then frame them with borders cut to size. You can also add more borders to enlarge the quilt further; see the *Great Border Tips*, page 38. Just remember that the length of each edge will be a multiple of 5″ (width of each center block; also the width of each pair of border strips).

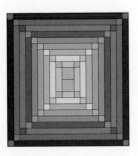   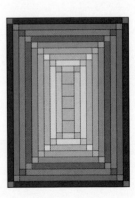

Palette and color arrangement both influence the overall effect of this pattern. You can choose a monochromatic, analogous, or high contrast scheme. You can also change the way the colors are placed or repeated to emphasize concentric bands, quadrants, or the X made by the corner squares.

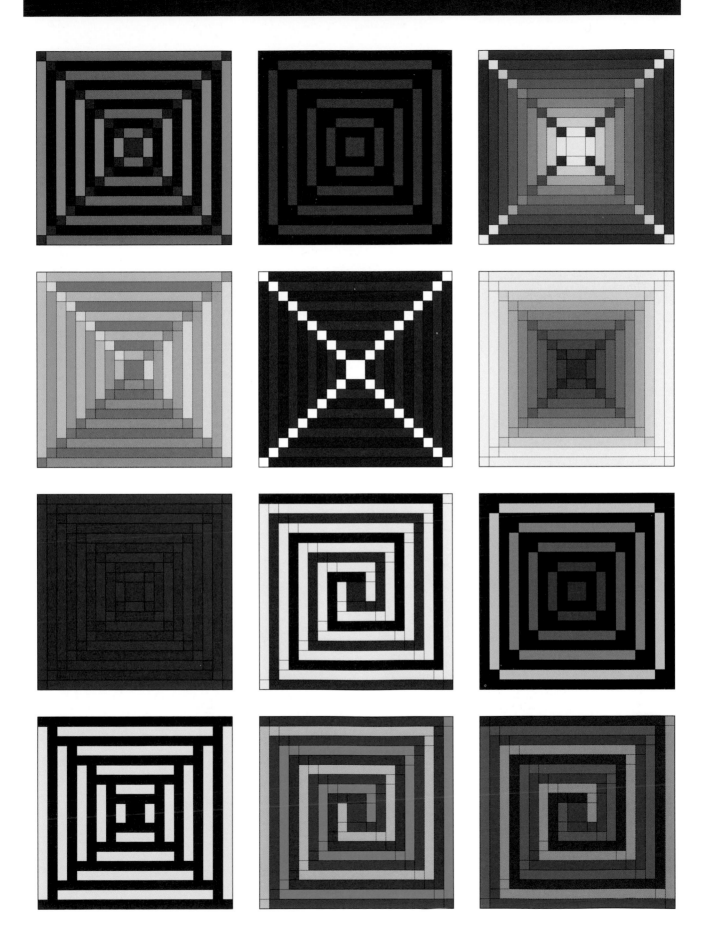

A Tufted Quilt

This lovely scrap quilt is about a hundred years old. It is simply classic nine-patch blocks set on point with alternate plain squares. The quilt top is tufted, or tied, to the backing with cotton yarn and it has a homey, informal look. Note that there are nine ties on each plain block, placed to correspond to those on the pieced ones. The arrangement of the nine-patch blocks is random. The pattern is so familiar and easy to duplicate in any size, directions for the patchwork are not included here.

When to Tuft

Tufting requires minimal marking and is faster to stitch than fancier quilting, so one of the primary reasons to use it is to save time. Sometimes called tying, it is traditionally used on informal quilts, particularly those made from wool, and on quilts where the patchwork is an allover pattern of small pieces, with no plain areas to showcase elaborate stitching. Both log cabin and crazy quilts are good candidates for tufting. Tufting is also a good technique to choose if you are making a fluffy comforter, as it will not flatten the loft of a thick batting.

Where to Tuft

Tying can be done at strategic design points on the quilt top (corners or centers of blocks or strips, for example) or in an allover geometric design, such as a square grid, with no reference to the patchwork pattern. Ties are generally spaced 3″ to 6″ apart, although one at each block intersection should be sufficient with today's battings, which do not separate into lumps over time.

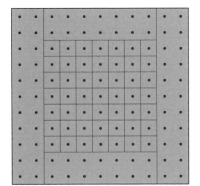
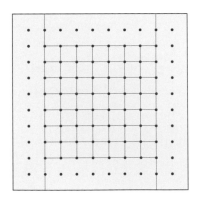
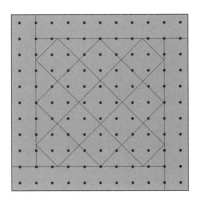

You can tie from either the quilt front or back, depending on whether or not you want the knots and thread ends to show. Likewise, you can tie with matching or contrasting thread or yarn which you can trim short or long as the piece requires. If you are making a wallhanging, consider adding strategically placed buttons or beads as you tie.

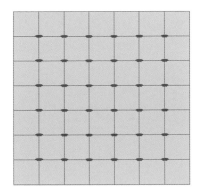
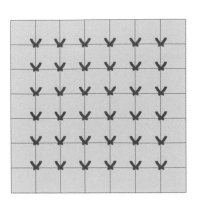

When choosing batting and thread for tufting, you must decide what effect you are trying to achieve. Do you want a fluffy quilt or one with a low loft? How apparent do you want the ties to be; should they blend or contrast with the fabrics? Is the quilt going on the bed or the wall? How often will it be laundered?

Batting

Because tufting is not dense like finely stitched quilting, it will not add stiffness to your quilt. To take advantage of this, choose batting with a soft hand, or drape, that is compatible with the weight of your quilt top. You can use batting that is either bonded or needle-punched. You can also use a flannel sheet or a blanket. If you are making a comforter, do not try to fill it with feathers or down, as the ties will not prevent them from drifting out of place.

Needles and Thread

Choose thread that complements the weight and style of your quilt, and that can be cleaned in the same manner. For lightweight fabrics you might use crochet cotton or fine cotton or linen yarn, or #5 or #8 pearl cotton. You could even use very fine ribbon, or, for a small, elegant piece, buttonhole twist. For heavier fabrics, candlewick yarn or #3 pearl cotton works well; for wool, use baby or sportweight yarn.

Use an embroidery or crewel needle large enough to hold your thread, but no larger than necessary to pass easily through the layers, to prevent leaving noticeable holes in the fabric.

If your tufting design is based upon the intersection of patchwork pieces, you do not need to mark the quilt top. If not, you may be able to gauge the placement by eye or with a ruler as you work. Otherwise, mark the design on the quilt top first, then assemble, layer and baste the quilt layers in the same manner as for conventional quilting. Thread your needle with one or more 36″ lengths of thread.

1. Make a single ¼"-long running stitch through all layers of the quilt at the location to be tufted, leaving a 3" thread end.

2. Make a single backstitch through the same holes formed by the running stitch; do not cut the thread.

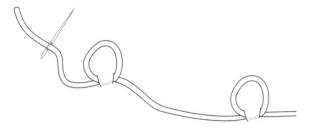

3. Make another running stitch and backstitch at the next and all subsequent locations to be tufted until the length of thread is used up.

4. Clip halfway between adjacent stitches and trim the ends if more than 3". Tie each pair of thread ends in a square knot. Trim ends evenly to between ¼" and 1".

GREAT DESIGN IDEAS

Use tufting to make a small wholecloth quilt for a pillow top, doll bed, or wallhanging. Begin with solid fabric and tie it with contrasting thread; to create an interesting pattern, use several colors of thread and/or vary the spacing of the ties. To plan your design, tape tracing paper over graph paper, then plot the desired pattern with colored pencils. Here are some examples of patterns you could create working with an evenly spaced grid of ties.

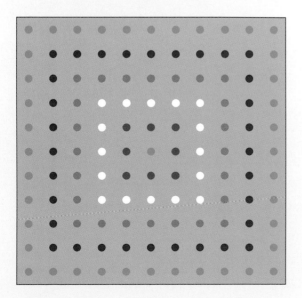 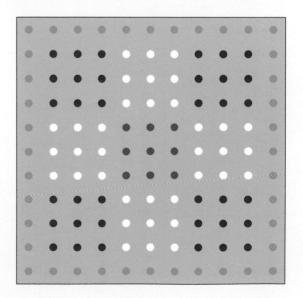

Country Coverlet

$\mathcal{O}$ne simple block in a positive/negative repeat gives this charming old quilt the look of an overshot woven coverlet. We will never know whether the quiltmaker used three different ginghams by choice or necessity, but whatever her reason, their random placement adds to the comfortable, homey effect of the patchwork. To make a very contemporary version of this quilt, use more colors to emphasize the zigzag diagonal in the overall pattern; see Changing Colors on page 54.

Note: All dimensions are finished size. This quilt is a nonstandard size. It may be big enough for a double bed if you turn it sideways—use the length of the quilt across the width of the bed. Amounts for full/queen are given in parentheses.

NEGATIVE BLOCK
28 (36) negative blocks, 10½″ square

POSITIVE BLOCK
28 (36) positive blocks, 10½″ square

BORDER
Four 3″-wide border strips, cut to size; side pieces added before top and bottom pieces

BINDING
Self-binding

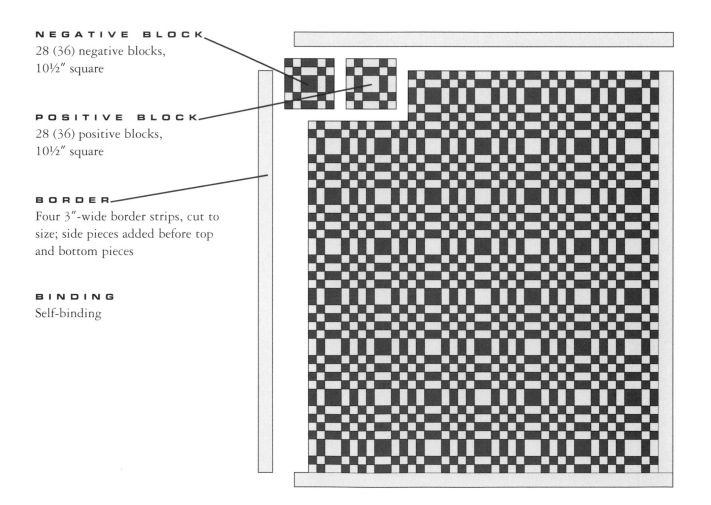

Yardages are based on 44″-wide fabric. Prepare templates, if desired, referring to drafting schematics. Cut strips and patches following cutting schematics and charts. See the *Great Piecing Tips*, page 50, for an alternate method of cutting and piecing. Except for drafting schematics, which give finished sizes, all dimensions include ¼″ seam allowance and strips include extra length, unless otherwise stated. (Note: Angles on all patches are 90°.)

DIMENSIONS

FINISHED BLOCK
10½″ square;
about 14¾″ diagonal

FINISHED QUILT
79½″ × 90″ (90″ × 100½″)

MATERIALS

ECRU SOLID
7¼ (8¾) yds.; see the *Great Fabric-Saving Tips*, below.

NAVY/WHITE CHECK
4½ (5¾) yds.

SELF-BINDING
No extra fabric or cutting required.

BACKING*
8 (9) yds.; see also the *Great Fabric-Saving Tips*, below.

BATTING*

THREAD

*Backing and batting should be cut and pieced as necessary so they are at least 4″ larger than quilt on all sides, then trimmed to size after quilting.

DRAFTING SCHEMATICS
(No seam allowance added)

A   1¾″
1¾″

B   1¾″
3½″

C   3½″
3½″

CUTTING SCHEMATICS
(Seam allowance included)

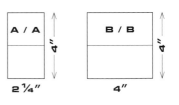

A / A   4″
2¼″

B / B   4″
4″

C   4″
4″

GREAT FABRIC-SAVING TIPS

You can reduce the yardage needed for this quilt if you use ecru solid for the backing and cut both the backing and border from the same 8 (9) yd. length of fabric. For the entire quilt you will need a total of 12 (14¼) yds. of ecru solid.

FIRST CUT			SECOND CUT			
				Number of Pieces		
Fabric and Yardage	Number of Pieces	Size	Method	For 28 (36) Positive Blocks	For 28 (36) Negative Blocks	Shape
STRIP-PIECED PATCHES*						
Ecru Solid and Navy/White Check 4 (5) yds. each	29 (36)	2¼" × 40"		224 (288)	224 (288)	A/A
	29 (36)	2¼" × 40"				
	23 (29)	2¼" × 40"		112 (144)	112 (144)	B/B
	23 (29)	2¼" × 40"				
* Join strips lengthwise as shown.						

FIRST CUT			SECOND CUT			
			Number of Pieces			
Fabric and Yardage	Number of Pieces	Size	For 28 (36) Positive Blocks	For 28 (36) Negative Blocks	Shape	
PLAIN PATCHES						
Ecru Solid ½ (¾) yd.	3 (4)	4" × 40"	28 (36)	—	C	
Navy/White Check ½ (¾) yd.	3 (4)	4" × 40"	—	28 (36)	C	

Fabric and Yardage	Number of Pieces	Size
BORDER*		
Ecru Solid 2¾ (3) yds.	2	3½" × 86" (3½" × 96")
	2	3½" × 90" (3½" × 101")
* See the *Great Fabric-Saving Tips*, opposite.		

You may find it quicker to make the blocks for the Country Coverlet by strip-piecing block units as shown below instead of cutting and joining smaller pieced and plain 9-patch units. Only two different pieced bands are needed to cut the four units that make up both the positive and negative blocks.

POSITIVE BAND

NEGATIVE BAND

1. From ecru solid cut **40 (52)** strips, **2¼" × 40"**, and **10 (13)** strips, **4" × 40".** Cut an equal number of strips from navy/white check.

2. Join strips as shown to make **10 (13)** positive bands and **10 (13)** negative bands.

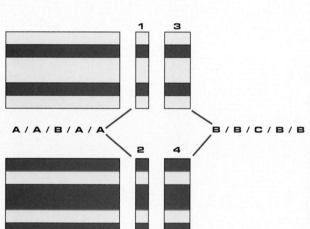

A / A / B / A / A   B / B / C / B / B

3. Cut bands into strips to make **112 (144)** each of **2¼"**-wide units **#1** and **#2.** Cut **28 (36)** each of **4"**-wide units **#3** and **#4.**

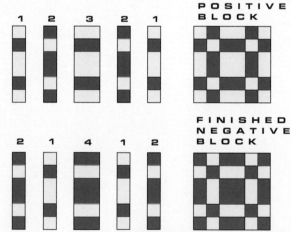

FINISHED POSITIVE BLOCK

FINISHED NEGATIVE BLOCK

4. Join units as shown to make **28 (36)** positive blocks and **28 (36)** negative blocks.

The size of this quilt can be adjusted easily from twin to full/queen by increasing the number of blocks to make one additional row and one additional column. Refer to the cutting charts, page 49, for the number of pieces to cut for the different sizes.

TWIN
56 blocks in a 7 × 8 layout

FULL/QUEEN
72 blocks in an 8 × 9 layout

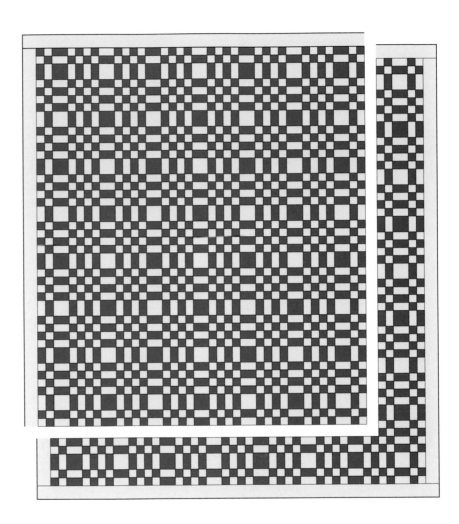

GREAT SIZING TIPS

Because this pattern will repeat continuously no matter how many blocks are placed in each row or column, you can plan your quilt to be almost any size you wish. Just remember that the length of each edge will be a multiple of 10½" (one block) plus 6" (the width of a pair of border strips).

    4 blocks in a 2 x 2 layout = 27"-square wallhanging

    9 blocks in a 3 x 3 layout = 37½"-square wallhanging

    15 blocks in a 3 x 5 layout = 37½" x 58½" crib quilt

Positive and Negative Blocks

Directions are given below for making one positive block; see also the *Great Piecing Tips*, page 50. Amounts for making all 28 (twin) or 36 (full/queen) positive blocks at the same time are given in parentheses. Rotate the pieced units and join them to dark C's to make the same number of negative blocks.

1. Sew A/A's together in pairs, alternating colors, to make 4 (112) (144) four-patches.

2. Arrange units as shown. Join units to make 3 rows. Join rows.

FINISHED POSITIVE BLOCK

FINISHED NEGATIVE BLOCK

Quilt Center

Arrange blocks as shown, alternating positive and negative blocks. Join blocks to make rows. Join rows.

TWIN

FULL/QUEEN

Border

Join border to quilt center, first long strips at sides, then short strips at top and bottom.

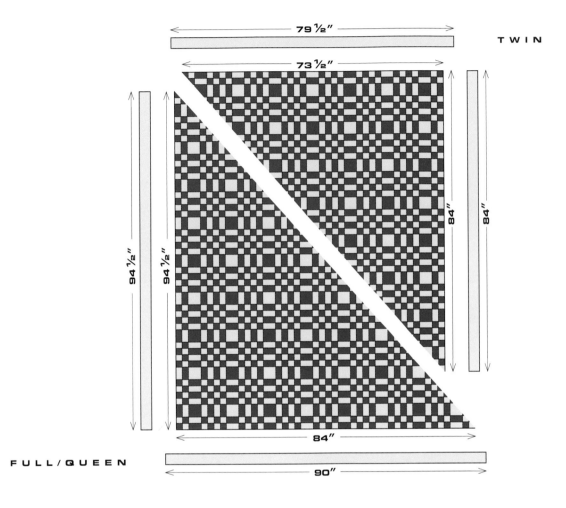

TWIN

FULL/QUEEN

Finishing

1. Mark quilting designs on quilt top.

◆ *For quilt center:* Mark an allover on-point square grid, using corners of patches as a guide.

◆ *For border:* Mark lines ¼″ and 1½″ from inner border seam all around.

2. Prepare batting and backing.

3. Assemble quilt layers.

4. Quilt on all marked lines.

5. Trim backing even with quilt top. Trim batting ¼″ smaller than fabric layers.

6. For self-binding, press fabric edges ¼″ to inside. Slipstitch quilt top and backing together along folds.

This pattern is at once familiar and unusual, and your use of color can turn it from classic to contemporary. It holds all sorts of secondary patterns that emerge with careful placement of contrasting color—have fun, but keep in mind that as the simple blocks become more complex, our directions may need some modification.

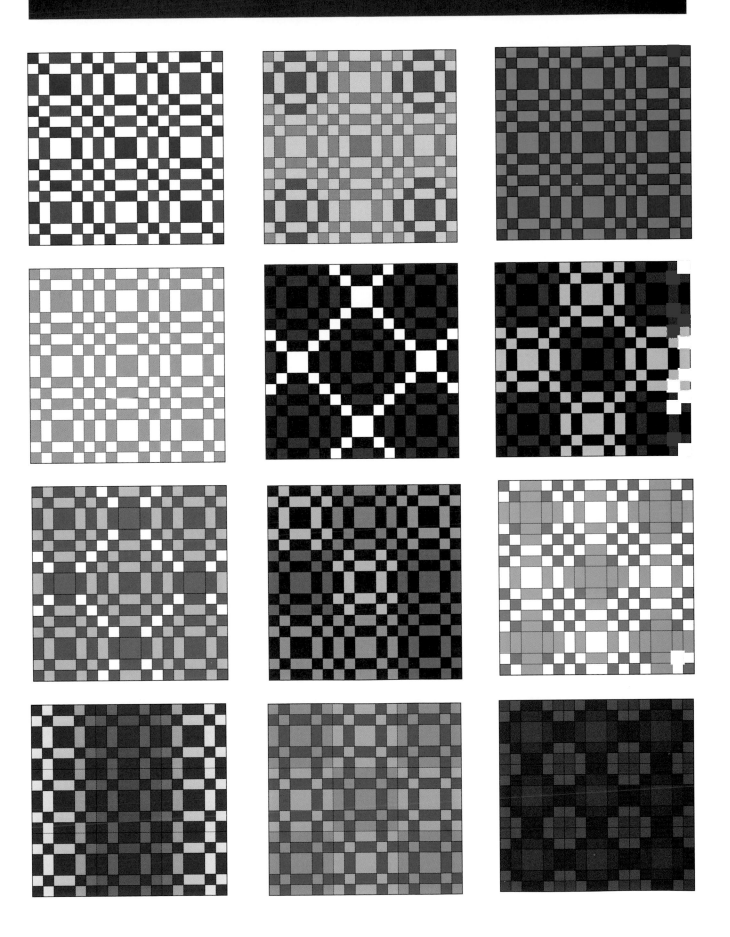

Prism Patches

$\mathscr{I}$t is not true that there is nothing new under the sun. Although squares and rectangles are the units with which so many classic and beloved quilt patterns are composed, we were determined to put them together in an original manner. Here we've created an uneven 9-patch and set it spinning. The throw pillows recombine the units in various ways. Compare this block with the Country Coverlet block on page 46—perhaps what goes around, comes around, after all.

Note: All dimensions except for binding are finished size. We have selected a representative color to depict the 13 bright solids on this quilt. Refer to the photographs, opposite and on page 65, to see the actual colors and their distribution.

PLAIN BLOCK
6 plain blocks, 6″ square

PIECED BLOCK
12 pieced blocks, 6″ square

CORNER TRIANGLE
4 corner triangles, about 4¼″ on two sides, 6″ on third side

SETTING TRIANGLE
10 setting triangles, 6″ on two sides, about 8½″ on third side

FIRST BORDER
Four 1¼″-wide pieced strips; side pieces added before top and bottom pieces

SECOND BORDER
Four 3½″-wide strips, cut to size; side pieces added before top and bottom pieces

THIRD BORDER
Four 1¼″-wide pieced strips; side pieces added before top and bottom pieces

BINDING
1¼″-wide strip, pieced as necessary and cut to size

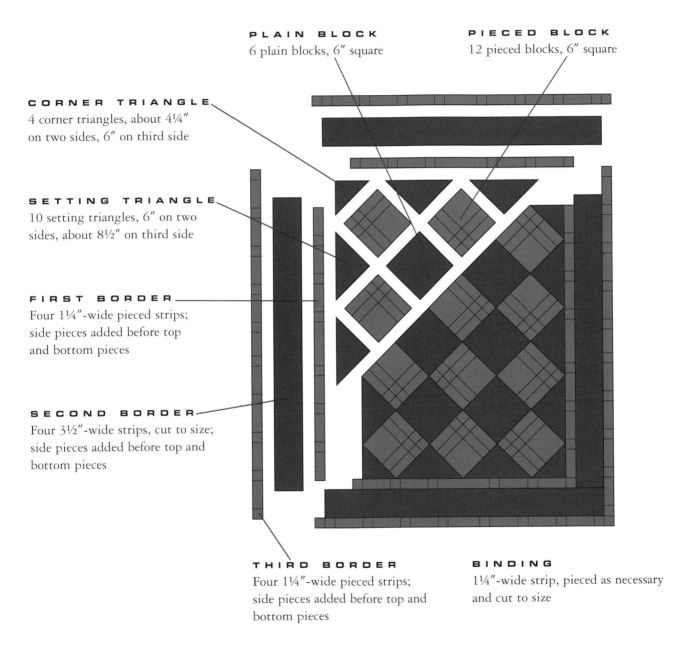

Yardages are based on 44″-wide fabric. Prepare templates, if desired, referring to drafting schematics. Cut strips and patches following cutting schematics and chart. Cut binding as directed below. Except for drafting schematics, which give finished sizes, all dimensions include ¼″ seam allowance and strips include extra length, unless otherwise stated. (Note: Angles on all patches are either 45° or 90°.)

DIMENSIONS

FINISHED PLAIN BLOCK
6″ square; about 8½″ diagonal

FINISHED PIECED BLOCK
6″ square; about 8½″ diagonal

FINISHED QUILT
About 37½″ × 46″

GREAT BINDING TIPS

If you want to make bias binding, you will need an additional ¼ yd. of black solid. Cut strips on a 45° diagonal and piece as needed.

MATERIALS

ASSORTED SOLIDS
¼ yd. each of 13 different bright solids, chosen from among shades of yellow, orange, red, blue, green, purple, and tan; see the *Great Planning Tips*, page 60.

BLACK SOLID
1¾ yds.

BINDING
Use ¼ yd. black solid, cut and pieced, to make a 1¼″ × 180″ straight-grain strip.

BACKING *
3 yds.

BATTING *

THREAD

*Backing and batting should be cut and pieced as necessary so they are at least 4″ larger than quilt on all sides, then trimmed to size after quilting.

DRAFTING SCHEMATICS
(No seam allowance added)

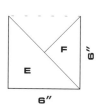

CUTTING SCHEMATICS

(Seam allowance included)

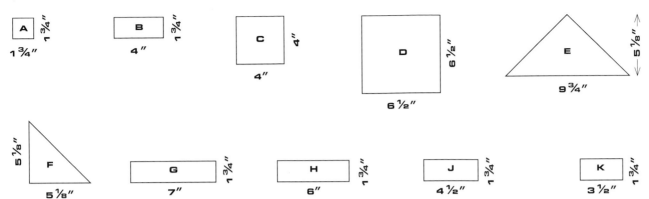

FIRST CUT			SECOND CUT			
			Number of Pieces			
Fabric and Yardage	Number of Pieces	Size	For Quilt Center	For First Border	For Third Border	Shape
PATCHES						
Assorted Solids ¼ yd. each	13	1¾" × 20"	48	24	40	A[1]
	13	1¾" × 40"	48	20	28	B[2]
	—	—	12	—	—	C[3]
	1	1¾" × 20"	—	2	—	G[4]
	1	1¾" × 20"	—	2	—	H[4]
	1	1¾" × 10"	—	—	2	J[4]
	1	1¾" × 10"	—	—	2	K[4]
Black Solid [5] 1½ yds.	1	6½" × 40"	6	—	—	D
	2	5⅛" × 40"	10	—	—	E
	1	5⅛" × 40"	4	—	—	F
SECOND BORDER						
	2	4" × 45"				
	2	4" × 47"				

[1] Cut one strip from each of 13 different solids. Cut 8 or 9 A's from each strip to total 112.
[2] Cut one strip from each of 13 different solids. Cut 7 or 8 B's from each strip to total 96.
[3] Cut one C from each of 12 different solids.
[4] Cut G's, H's, J's, and K's from 8 different solids.
[5] Cut all strips on lengthwise grain.

The placement of bright solids on this quilt may appear at first glance to be totally random, but a closer look reveals the careful planning that went into creating that effect; see the photographs on pages 56 and 65 for the actual placement and distribution of colors.

The designer used a total of 13 different bright solids on her quilt, but the design could work as easily with 12 (the number of pieced blocks in the quilt center). If you study the design, you will notice that each of the pieced blocks is made of 9 patches cut from 9 different colors, and each of the large squares in these blocks is a different color. The center patches on the four sides of both pieced borders were cut from 8 different colors, as were the 8 corner squares. Even the trios of small squares in the corners of the outer pieced border were cut from 12 different colors. In general, no two patches of the same bright solid touch on any side or corner. Notice also that the orientation of individual pieced blocks is not repeated in any horizontal or vertical row they form.

Use the diagram on page 67 to plan your quilt. After all of your patches have been cut out, lay them out to be sure you are satisfied with the arrangement of the bright colors before doing any stitching.

LARGE SQUARES

BORDER CENTER PATCHES

CORNER SQUARES

CORNER TRIOS

Note: Directions are given below for making one pieced block; see the Great Planning Tips, *opposite.*
Amounts for making all 12 pieced blocks at the same time are given in parentheses.

Pieced Block

1. Join 4 A's to make one (12) 4-patch.

2. Join 4 (98) B's in pairs.

3. Arrange units as shown. Join units to make 2 rows. Join rows.

FINISHED PIECED BLOCK

Quilt Center

Arrange units as shown. Join units to make rows. Join rows.

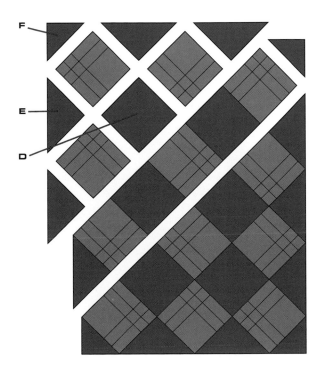

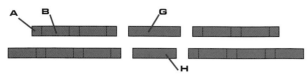

Borders

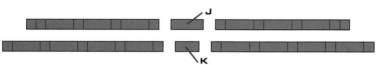

1. Assemble pieced first border; see also the *Great Pieced-Border Tips*, below.

◆ Join A's and B's as shown to make 4 short strips and 4 long strips.

◆ Stitch G's between pairs of short strips and H's between pairs of long strips.

◆ Join border to quilt center, first long strips at sides, then short strips at top and bottom.

2. Join plain second border to quilt, first long strips at sides, then short strips at top and bottom.

3. Assemble pieced third border.

◆ Join A's and B's as shown to make 4 short strips and 4 long strips.

◆ Stitch J's between pairs of short strips and K's between pairs of long strips.

◆ Join border to quilt, first long strips at sides, then short strips at top and bottom.

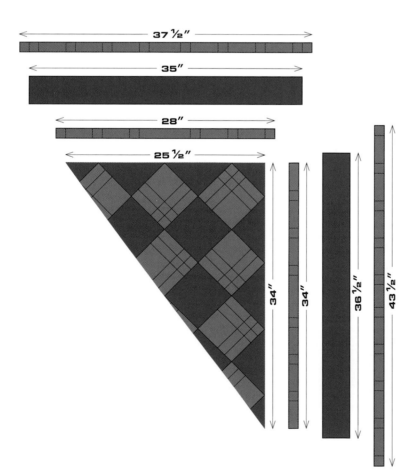

GREAT PIECED-BORDER TIPS

You can ensure that your pieced borders will fit your quilt exactly by adjusting the center patches G, H, J, and K.

Cut the center patches about 3″ longer than indicated on the cutting schematics, page 59. Assemble the ends of each border strip, then trim its center patch so that when it is stitched between the strip ends the resulting border strip will be the same length as the quilt edge to which it will be joined.

Finishing

1. Mark quilting designs on quilt top.
- *For **quilt center:*** Mark motifs on plain blocks and setting triangles only, placing lines 1″ and 2″ from seams. Mark a line on each corner triangle between long edge and opposite corner.
- *For **second border:*** Mark on-point squares, centered between long seams: Mark a 1¾″ square in each corner, ½″ from seams, then mark seven 1½″ squares on each half of top and bottom border strips, working from large corner squares in toward center; mark center square, sized as necessary to fit. Mark border sides in same manner, making nine 1½″ squares on each side of center.

2. Prepare batting and backing.
3. Assemble quilt layers.
4. Quilt in-the-ditch on all seams of pieced blocks and on inner and outer edges of pieced borders. Quilt on all marked lines.

5. Trim batting and backing to ⅜″ beyond outermost seam line.
6. Bind quilt edges.

GREAT SIZING IDEAS

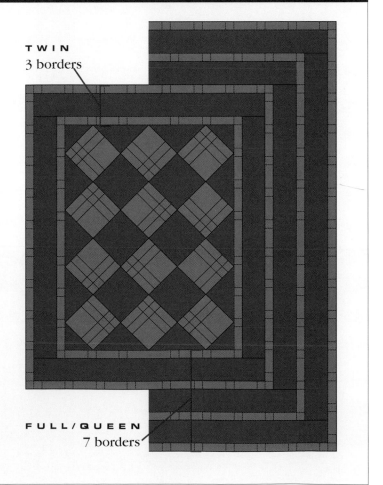

If you double the size of the wallhanging components (enlarge them to 200%), they will be just the right size to make a 75″ x 92″ twin coverlet. To enlarge the quilt to 94″ x 111″ for full/queen, add four more borders to the twin coverlet, continuing the pattern of alternating plain and pieced borders.

For the twin, you will need about four times as much fabric as for the wallhanging. For the full/queen, you will need four times the fabric as for the wallhanging, plus an extra 3 yds. of black solid to make the additional plain borders.

TWIN
3 borders

FULL/QUEEN
7 borders

The components that make up the Prism Patches wallhanging can be recombined to create many different designs. All of the pillows shown below can easily be made from fabric left over from the wallhanging. Try making one or more of our pillows or design your own. Use any or all of the components from the wallhanging and add any new elements as necessary.

Pillow #1 (15½″ square finished size) is made of 9 black C's framed with sashing composed of assorted color A's and B's. Pillow #2 (also 15½″ square) is made of one assorted color pieced block, 4 black C's, 4 new black rectangles, and sashing made of assorted color A's, B's, and 4 new color rectangles. Pillow #3 (12″ square) has no black units at all and is made of 4 assorted color pieced blocks.

Follow the cutting chart for the number of patches to cut for each pillow, or cut your patches based on a graph paper pattern of your own design.

Piece together the pillow top, then assemble the layers and quilt in-the-ditch on all seams or as desired. Add a pillow back and corded piping, and stuff firmly with fiberfill; for the larger pillows, you can insert a 16″-square knife-edge pillow form instead.

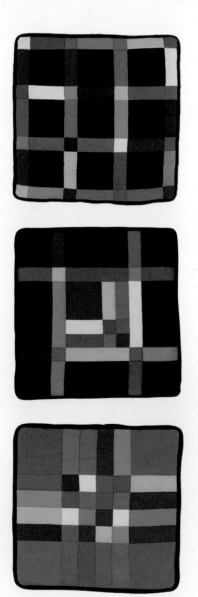

PILLOW		
Fabric and Yardage	Number of Pieces	Size/Shape
FOR PILLOW #1 (BLACK BLOCKS WITH SASHING)		
Assorted Solids	16	A
	24	B
Black Solid	9	C
FOR PILLOW #2 (BLACK AND ASSORTED COLOR BLOCKS WITH SASHING)		
Assorted Solids	8	A
	12	B
	4	2″ × 6½″
Black Solid	4	C
	4	4″ × 6½″
FOR PILLOW #3 (ASSORTED COLOR BLOCKS)		
Assorted Solids	16	A
	16	B
	4	C

YYou can have a lot of fun planning colors for this quilt, which can spin from childlike to sophisticated with your palette. To give it a quiet look, use only cool colors, or nine or more values of any one color. To give it a classic air, use no more than three colors. Try repeating the background color in the innermost small square patch.

Photocopy this page, then create your own color scheme using colored pencils or markers. Refer to the examples shown, or design a unique arrangement to match your decor or please your fancy. See what happens when adjacent corners of the pieced blocks are the same color.

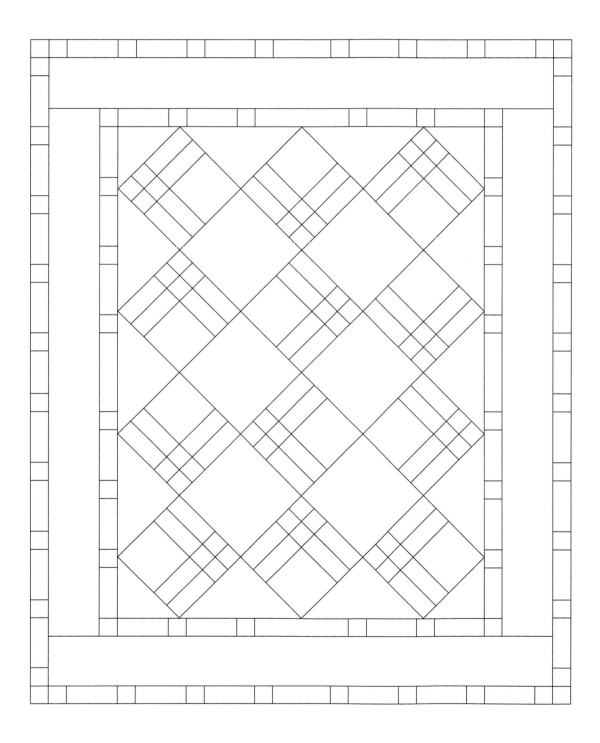

If you turn all of the pieced blocks in one direction, this pattern will be less exuberant. Omitting the plain blocks will create interesting allover patterns. Note how different a simple straight set variation appears to your eye, and how sashing changes the balance. Redistribute your colors to enhance any of these variations.

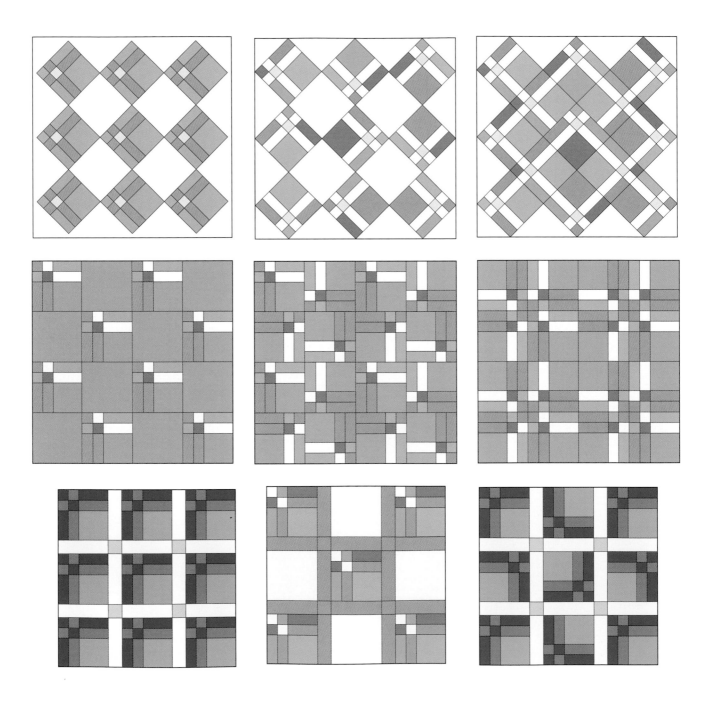

Honor to the 9-Patch

Perhaps because it combines simplicity with a sometimes surprising versatility, the basic 9-patch pattern—nine identical squares arranged in a 3 x 3 grid— is an enduring favorite. Many a beginning quilter's first project has been a simple two-tone 9-patch quilt, and sophisticated designers continue to find fresh and unexpected ways to use this well-loved block. Indeed, many of the blocks in this book can be seen as variations on the basic 9-patch, such as Prism Patches on page 56. The nine sections of the block can be resized to include both squares and rectangles, and any or all of these can be subdivided into 3-, 4-, or 9-patches, or myriad other patterns—but as long as the characteristic configuration of two horizontal and two vertical seams forming a grid remains, the block is still a 9-patch and can be assembled as such.

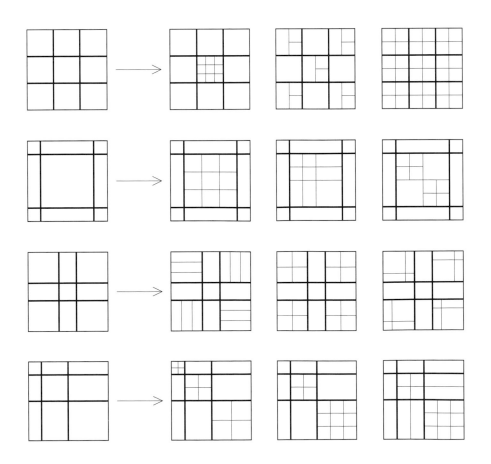

The placement and balance of color can change the look of a 9 patch block, defining a regular two-tone checkerboard or creating a dynamic multicolor arrangement whose complete pattern appears only after several blocks have been joined. Look at other *Changing Colors* pages in this book to see the effect of positive/negative block arrangement and of plain alternate blocks with different 9-patch colorations.

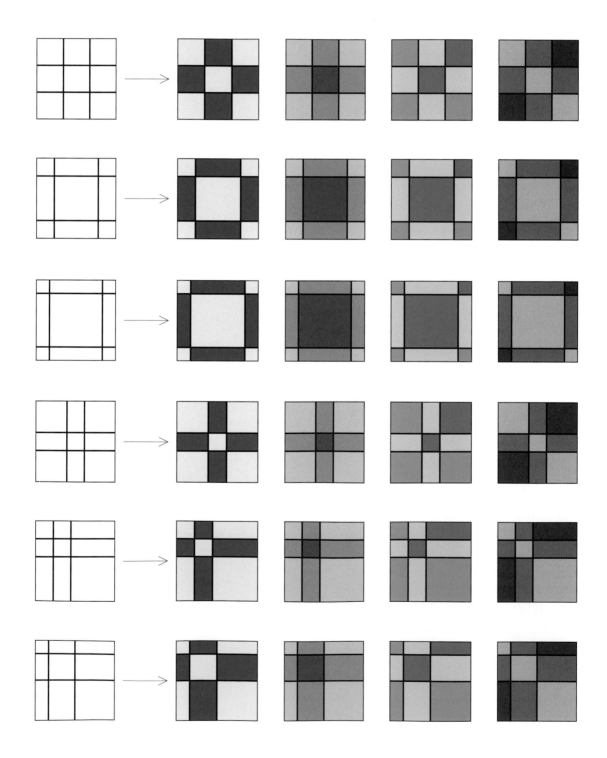

It's hard to go wrong setting 9-patch blocks. Whether you alternate them with plain blocks, repeat them one against another, set them squarely or on point, you will have a pleasing quilt. Depending upon the block variation with which you are working, a simple set may be all you need to create an apparently complex pattern. Consider as well developing an irregular repetition of blocks to create a larger overall pattern.

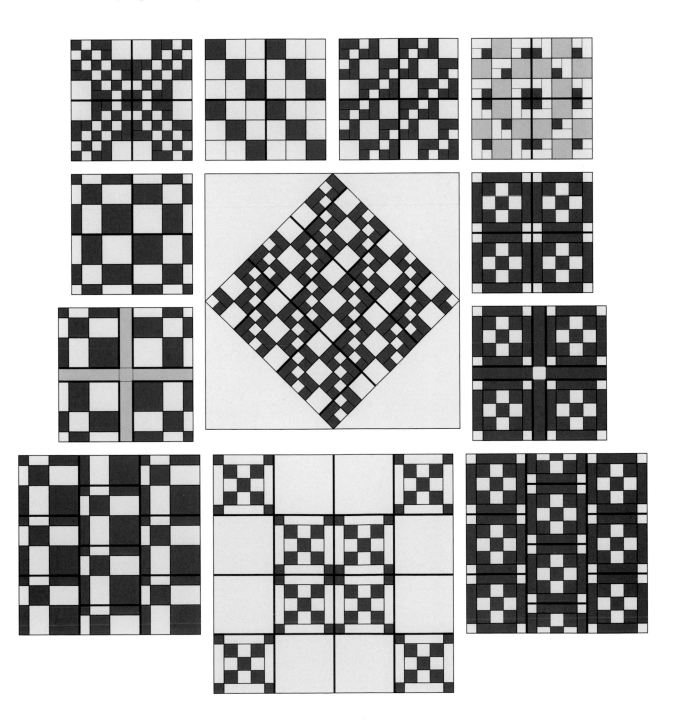

Tree of Paradise

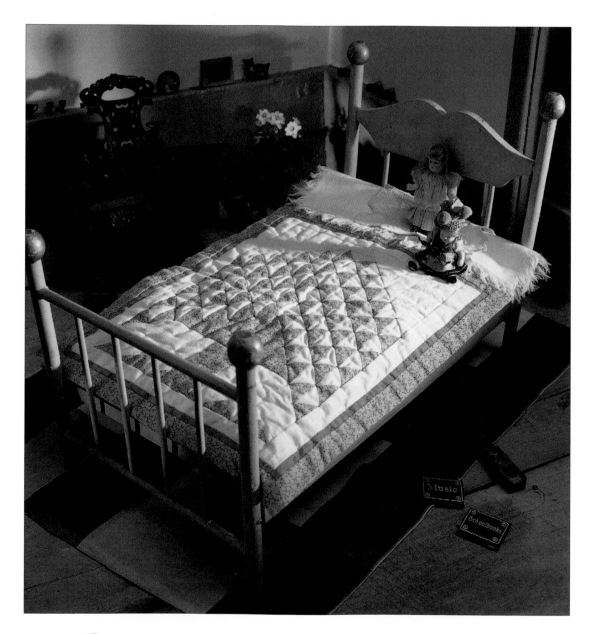

$\mathcal{S}$mall is the word for this quilt, and Patience was its maker. Strip-pieced triangle squares help with the sewing, but tiny pieces are always tricky. However, you need only one block of this old pattern to cover a doll bed, so don't think of this as a lifetime project. We've dipped new muslin and quaint calico in tea to give this quilt a little history; tufts of embroidery floss add a pretty pattern to the plain pink back.

Note: All dimensions are finished size.

BLOCK
One block,
9″ × 13¾″

FIRST BORDER
Four ⅝″-wide strips, cut to size;
top and bottom pieces added
before side pieces

SECOND BORDER
Four ¼″-wide strips, cut to size;
top and bottom pieces added
before side pieces

THIRD BORDER
Four ⅞″-wide strips, cut to size;
top and bottom pieces added
before side pieces

BINDING
Self-binding

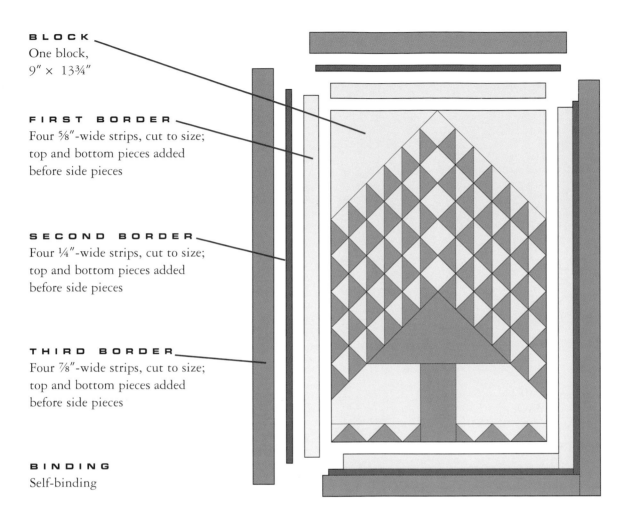

GREAT SIZING TIPS

If you triple the size of the components (enlarge them to 300%), you can make a 37½″ x 51¾″ crib quilt. You will need about 6 times as much fabric for the large quilt as for the small one.

Yardages are based on 44″-wide fabric. Prepare templates, if desired, referring to drafting schematics; make one template for both A and B/B. Cut strips and patches following cutting schematics and charts, and the *Great Cutting Tips* on page 76. Except for drafting schematics, which give finished sizes, all dimensions include ¼″ seam allowance and strips include extra length, unless otherwise stated.
(Note: Unmarked angles on cutting schematics are either 45° or 90°.)

DIMENSIONS

FINISHED BLOCK
9″ × 13¾″

FINISHED QUILT
12½″ × 17¼″

MATERIALS

MUSLIN SOLID
½ yd.

PINK PRINT
¼ yd.

OLIVE PRINT
½ yd.

SELF-BINDING
No extra fabric or cutting required.

BACKING*
¾ yd.

BATTING*

THREAD

FLOSS
Six-strand cotton embroidery floss, ecru and burgundy

*Backing and batting should be cut and pieced as necessary so they are at least 4″ larger than quilt on all sides, then trimmed to size after quilting.

DRAFTING SCHEMATICS
(No seam allowance added)

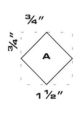

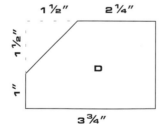

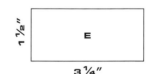

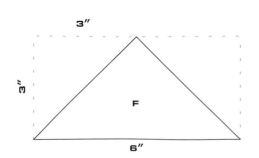

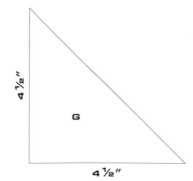

FIRST CUT			SECOND CUT	
Fabric and Yardage	Number of Pieces	Size	Number of Pieces	Shape
FIRST BORDER				
Muslin Solid * ½ yd.	1	1⅛″ × 30″	2	1⅛″ × 12″
	1	1⅛″ × 40″	2	1⅛″ × 16″
SECOND BORDER				
Pink Print ¼ yd.	1	¾″ × 30″	2	¾″ × 13″
	1	¾″ × 40″	2	¾″ × 19″
THIRD BORDER				
Olive Print* ½ yd.	1	1⅜″ × 30″	2	1⅜″ × 14″
	1	1⅜″ × 40″	2	1⅜″ × 20″
*Reserve remainder of fabric for cutting plain patches and strip-pieced triangle squares; see page 76.				

CUTTING SCHEMATICS

(Seam allowance included)

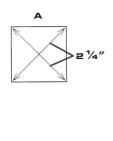

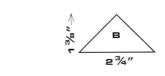

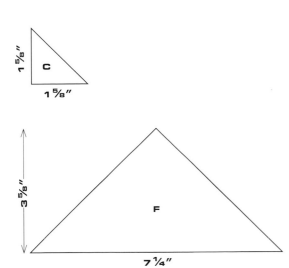

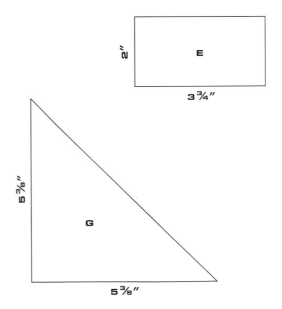

FIRST CUT			SECOND CUT		
Fabric and Yardage	Number of Pieces	Size	Method	Number of Pieces	Shape
STRIP-PIECED TRIANGLE SQUARES*					
Muslin Solid	8	2¾" × 10" (bias strip)		50	B/B
Olive Print	8	2¾" × 10" (bias strip)			

*See *Strip-Pieced Triangle Squares* on page 220. Use remainder of fabric from first and third borders. Join strips lengthwise in groups of eight, alternating colors as shown. Use template for cutting accurate squares.

FIRST CUT			SECOND CUT	
Fabric and Yardage	Number of Pieces	Size	Number of Pieces	Shape
PLAIN PATCHES[1]				
Muslin Solid	1	2" × 10"	5	A[2]
	1	1⅜" × 10"	4	B
	1	1⅝" square	2	C
	1	3" × 10"	1	D[3]
			1	D$_R$
	1	5⅜" square	2	G
Olive Print	1	1⅜" × 30"	14	B
	1	1⅝" square	2	C
	1	—	—	E
	1	—	—	F

[1] Use remainder of fabric from first and third borders.
[2] Extra width included. Use template for cutting accurate squares.
[3] Cut D and D$_R$ patches from same strip; see the *Great Cutting Tips* at right. Reverse template D on fabric to cut D$_R$.

GREAT CUTTING TIPS

A rotary cutter makes quick work of cutting accurate straight-edged patches. Glue a paper template to the underside of a clear plastic ruler as a guide.

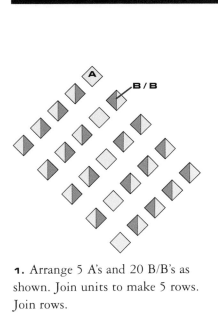

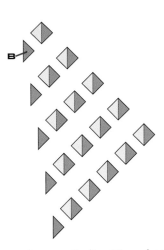

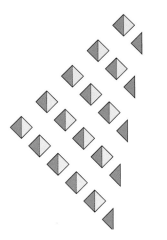

1. Arrange 5 A's and 20 B/B's as shown. Join units to make 5 rows. Join rows.

2. Arrange 5 olive B's and 15 B/B's as shown. Join units to make 5 rows. Join rows.

3. Join 5 olive B's and 15 B/B's to make reverse of piece from Step 2.

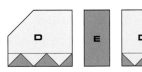

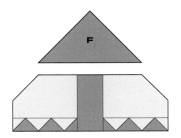

4. Join C's and B's as shown to make 2 strips.

5. Join D and D$_R$ to strips from Step 4. Join units to E.

6. Join F to piece from Step 5.

7. Arrange pieces from Steps 1, 2, 3, and 6 as shown. Join pieces to make 2 rows. Join rows.

8. Join G's to piece from Step 7.

FINISHED BLOCK

Borders

Join borders to quilt center, first short strips at top and bottom, then long strips at sides. Complete first border before proceeding to second, then third.

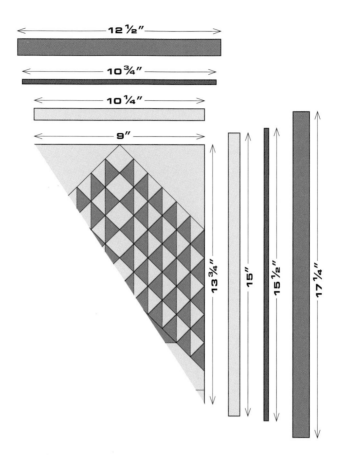

Finishing

1. Mark tufting design on quilt top.

◆ Align ruler with edges of A's and B/B's. Mark dots as shown. Outermost dots should be on seam between second and third borders.

2. Prepare batting and backing.

3. Assemble quilt layers.

4. Tuft the quilt; see *Tufting*, pages 232-233. Use burgundy floss to tie knots at corners of A's, B's, B/B's, and at dots marked on F. Tie with ecru at remaining dots.

5. Bind quilt edges.

◆ Trim batting even with outermost seam line of quilt top. Trim quilt top and backing to ¼" beyond batting.

◆ Press under ¼" at edges of quilt top and backing, align folds, and slipstitch together.

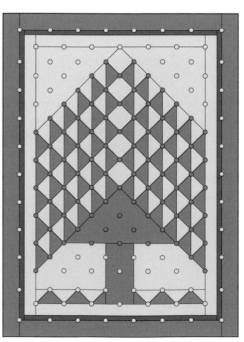

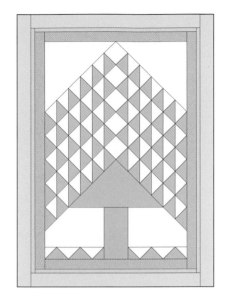

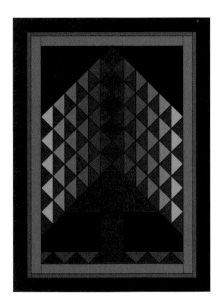

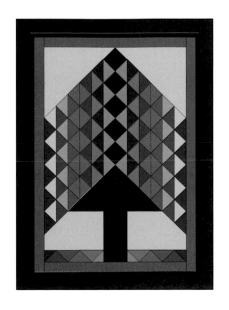

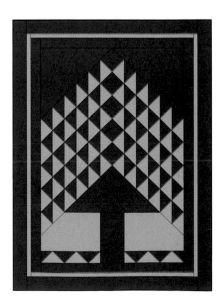

Kitty in the Corner

The elegance and simplicity of this pattern assure that it will never be out of vogue. Signed on the back by Cornelia Palmer, this exquisite chintz and muslin example dates from 1830. We admire this quilter not only for her lovely quilting and wonderful use of fabric, but also for her thrift and patience—many of the square and triangular patches are themselves pieced from small, and not always matching, bits of cloth. On the trunk, in a diagonally set version of the pattern, the 9-patch blocks alternate with contrasting plain blocks.

Note: All dimensions except for binding are finished size. This quilt is a nonstandard size. You might prefer to use the length of the quilt across the width of your bed. Amounts below are for full/queen. Differing amounts for twin are given in parentheses. We have selected a representative color to depict the assorted prints of the quilt center. Make about 13 (11) block centers each from mustard, blue, green, and brown prints to get a good mix. Refer to the photographs, opposite and on page 88, to see the actual distribution of colors.

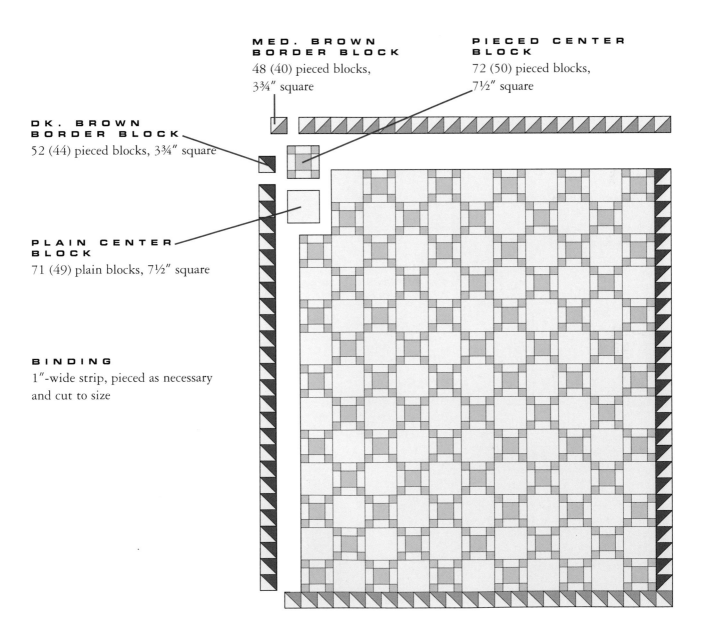

MED. BROWN BORDER BLOCK
48 (40) pieced blocks, 3¾″ square

PIECED CENTER BLOCK
72 (50) pieced blocks, 7½″ square

DK. BROWN BORDER BLOCK
52 (44) pieced blocks, 3¾″ square

PLAIN CENTER BLOCK
71 (49) plain blocks, 7½″ square

BINDING
1″-wide strip, pieced as necessary and cut to size

Note: Sizes and amounts below are for full/queen.
Differing sizes and amounts for twin are given in parentheses.

Yardages are based on 44″-wide fabric. Prepare templates, if desired, referring to drafting schematics. Cut strips and patches following cutting schematics and charts. Cut binding as directed below. Except for drafting schematics, which give finished sizes, all dimensions include ¼″ seam allowance and strips include extra length, unless otherwise stated. (Note: Angles on all patches are either 45° or 90°.)

DIMENSIONS

FINISHED CENTER BLOCK
7½″ square; about 10⅝″ diagonal

FINISHED BORDER BLOCK
3¾″ square; about 5¼″diagonal

FINISHED QUILT
90″ × 105″ (75″ × 90″)

MATERIALS

☐ **MUSLIN SOLID**
8¼ (6½) yds.

▨ **MED. BROWN PRINT**
¾ yd.

▩ **DK. BROWN PRINT**
¾ yd.

▧ **ASSORTED MUSTARD, BLUE, GREEN, AND BROWN PRINTS**
3 (2¾) yds. equally divided among at least 4 different colors

BINDING
Use ½ yd. muslin solid, cut and pieced, to make a 1″ × 400″ (1″ × 340″) straight-grain strip.

BACKING *
9¾ (8½) yds.

BATTING *

THREAD

*Backing and batting should be cut and pieced as necessary so they are at least 4″ larger than quilt on all sides, then trimmed to size after quilting.

DRAFTING SCHEMATICS

(No seam allowance added)

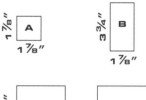

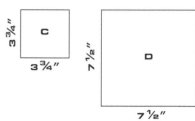

GREAT BINDING TIPS

If you want to make bias binding, you will need an additional ½ (¼) yd. of muslin solid. Cut strips on a 45° diagonal and piece as needed.

CUTTING SCHEMATICS

(Seam allowance included)

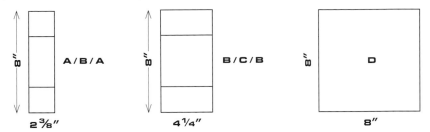

A/B/A — 8", 2⅜"

B/C/B — 8", 4¼"

D — 8", 8"

E — 4⅝", 4⅝"

FIRST CUT			SECOND CUT		
Fabric and Yardage	Number of Pieces	Size	Method	Number of Pieces	Shape
STRIP-PIECED PATCHES[1]					
Muslin Solid and Assorted Prints[2] 1½ yds. each	18 (14)	2⅜" × 40"		144 (100)	A/B/A
	9 (7)	4¼" × 40"			
Muslin Solid and Assorted Prints[2] 1¼ (1) yds. each	16 (12)	2⅜" × 40"		72 (50)	B/C/B
	8 (6)	4¼" × 40"			

[1]Join strips lengthwise, alternating colors as shown.
[2]Print strips should be evenly distributed among mustard, blue, green, and brown prints.

FIRST CUT			SECOND CUT	
Fabric and Yardage	Number of Pieces	Size	Number of Pieces	Shape
PLAIN PATCHES				
Muslin Solid 3½ (2½) yds.	15 (10)	8" × 40"	71 (49)	D
SPEEDY TRIANGLE SQUARES*				
Muslin Solid and Med. Brown Print ¾ yd. each	2	19½" square	48 (40)	E/E
Muslin Solid and Dk. Brown Print ¾ yd. each	2	19½" square	52 (44)	E/E

*See *Speedy Triangle Squares*, page 221. Mark 4 × 4 grids with 4⅝" squares.

The size of this quilt can be adjusted easily from full/queen to twin by decreasing the number of center blocks to make 2 fewer rows and 2 fewer columns, and decreasing the number of border blocks accordingly. Refer to the cutting charts on page 83 for the number of pieces to cut for the different sizes.

FULL/QUEEN
71 plain center blocks and 72 pieced center blocks in an 11 × 13 layout; quilt center 82½″ × 97½″

TWIN
49 plain center blocks and 50 pieced center blocks in a 9 × 11 layout; quilt center 67½″ × 82½″

Because this pattern will repeat continuously no matter how many blocks are placed in each row or column, you can plan your quilt to be almost any size you wish. Just remember that the length of each edge will be a multiple of 7½″ (width of each block; also the width of a pair of border strips). Some examples:

5 blocks in a 5 x 1 layout = 15″ x 45″ table runner

9 blocks in a 3 x 3 layout = 30″-square wallhanging

48 blocks in a 6 x 8 layout = 45″ x 60″ crib quilt

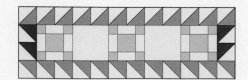

Pieced Center Block

Join units as shown to make one block. Make 72 blocks (full/queen) or 50 blocks (twin).

A/B/A   B/C/B

FINISHED PIECED
CENTER BLOCK

QUILT ASSEMBLY

Quilt Center

Arrange blocks as shown, alternating plain and pieced blocks; make sure the prints/colors are evenly distributed; refer to the photographs on pages 80 and 88 for color placement on our quilt. Join blocks to make rows. Join rows.

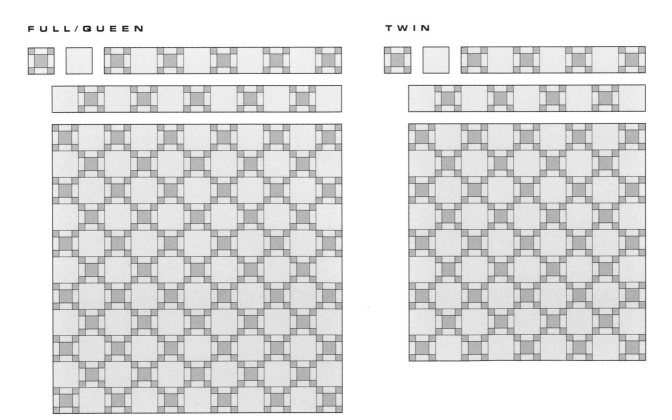

FULL/QUEEN

TWIN

Border

Directions are given below for full/queen. Differing amounts for twin are given in parentheses. Refer to the Components diagram on page 81 for orientation of triangle squares on all sides of quilt. Note that the top and bottom strips are mirror images, as are left- and right-side strips. See the *Great Border Tips*, below, for alternate corner settings.

1. Join 24 (20) muslin/med. brown E/E's to make 2 short strips.
2. Join 26 (22) of muslin/dk. brown E/E's to make 2 long strips.
3. Join border to quilt center, first long strips at sides, then short strips at top and bottom.

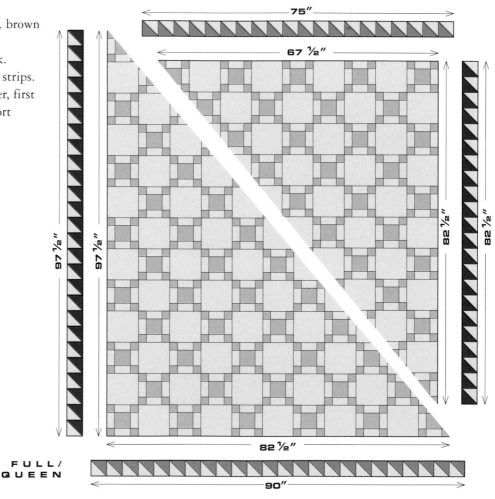

GREAT BORDER TIPS

On this antique quilt, all of the triangle squares in each border strip have the same orientation, which creates four different border corners. You can change the orientation of the end triangle squares of the top and bottom border strips to change the corner patterns.

86

Finishing

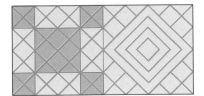

1. Mark quilting designs on quilt top.
- *For pieced center blocks:* Mark an allover on-point square grid, using corners of patches as a guide.
- *For plain center blocks:* Connect centers of sides to mark a large on-point square. Continue marking pattern of small grid squares in corners of plain block, stopping at large square. Mark lines for inward echo quilting inside large square as shown.

- *For border blocks:* Mark lines for inward echo quilting on muslin solid triangle in each block as shown. Do not mark brown triangles.
2. Prepare batting and backing.
3. Assemble quilt layers.
4. Quilt on all marked lines.
5. Trim batting and backing even with quilt top.
6. Bind quilt edges.

GREAT ACCESSORY IDEAS

You can make a 15″-square throw pillow, or a pair of them, from the components of the Kitty in the Corner quilt. Frame a block with triangle squares, then assemble the layers and quilt them. Add a pillow back and stuff with fiberfill, or insert a 15″-square knife-edge pillow form.

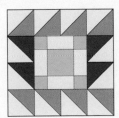

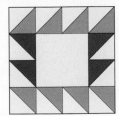

In this pattern, alternating pieced and plain blocks create a lattice; the fewer colors you use, the stronger the lattice will appear. Reversing or redistributing light and dark elements will alter the overall effect. Use a high-contrast palette for a traditional interpretation, or shade your hues subtly across the surface for one that is unique.

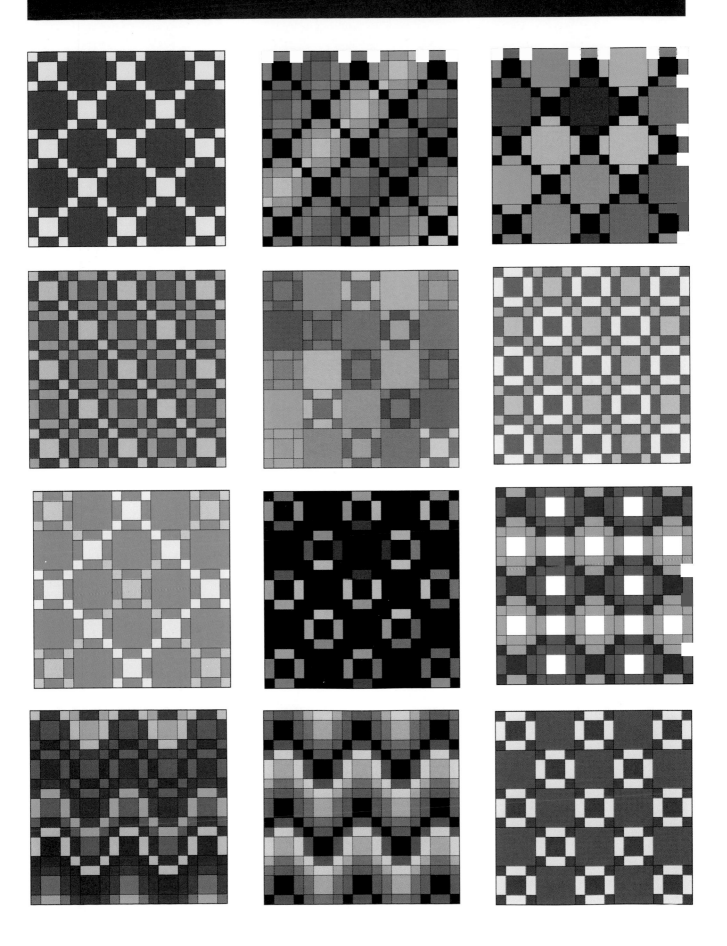

Chevron

$\mathscr{A}$t first glance, the perpendicularly butted rectangles of this colorful quilted table mat look like a Log Cabin variation. But, a closer look shows there is no way to assemble this pattern without sewing a considerable number of inside corners—thus making this project a challenge for even the most accomplished quilters. To see the beautiful antique quilt that inspired this keepsake pieced mat, turn to page 96.

Note: All dimensions except for binding are finished size.
We have selected a representative color to depict the assorted light, medium, and
dark blue prints of the quilt center. Refer to the photographs, opposite and on page 97,
to see the actual colors and their distribution.

BLOCK
One block, 11¾" square

FIRST BORDER
Four strips, two ¾" × 11¾"
and two ¾" × 13¼"; side pieces
added before top and bottom pieces

SECOND BORDER
Four strips, two 1⅝" × 13¼" and
two 1⅝" × 16½"; side pieces added
before top and bottom pieces

BINDING
1½"-wide strip, pieced as necessary
and cut to size

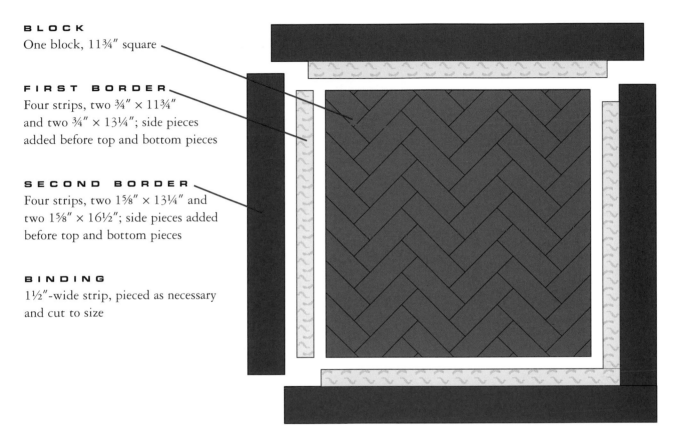

Yardages are based on 44"-wide fabric. Prepare template, if desired, referring to drafting schematic. Cut strips and patches following cutting schematic and chart. Cut binding as directed below. Except for drafting schematic, which gives finished size, all dimensions include ¼" seam allowance and strips include extra length, unless otherwise stated. (Note: Angles on all patches are 90°.)

DIMENSIONS

FINISHED BLOCK
11¾" square

FINISHED QUILT
16½" square

DRAFTING SCHEMATIC
(No seam allowance added)

1" × 3"

CUTTING SCHEMATIC
(Seam allowance included)

1½" × 3½"

MATERIALS

LT. BLUE-ON-ECRU PRINT
½ yd.

ASSORTED BLUE PRINTS
Small amounts of at least 20 different lt., med., and dk. blue prints to total about ½ yd.

DK. BLUE PRINT
¾ yd.

BINDING
Use remainder of fabric from first border, cut and pieced, to make a 1½" × 80" straight-grain strip.

BACKING *
¾ yd.

BATTING *

THREAD

*Backing and batting should be cut and pieced as necessary so they are at least 4" larger than quilt on all sides, then trimmed to size after quilting.

Fabric and Yardage	Number of Pieces	Size/Shape
PATCHES [1]		
Assorted Blue Prints ½ yd.	66	Rectangle 
FIRST BORDER [2]		
Lt. Blue-on-Ecru Print ½ yd.	2	1¼" × 12¼"
	2	1¼" × 13¾"
SECOND BORDER [3]		
Dk. Blue Print ¾ yd.	2	2⅛" × 13¾"
	2	2⅛" × 17"

[1] Cut an equal number of rectangles from each print.
[2] Strips are exact length. Reserve remainder of fabric for binding.
[3] Strips are exact length.

GREAT BINDING TIPS

If you want to make bias binding, you will need an additional ¼ yd. of lt. blue-on-ecru print. Cut strips on a 45° diagonal and piece as needed.

Block

Assemble block as directed; see the *Great Piecing Tips*, below, and the photographs on pages 90 and 97 for actual colors of rectangles and their distribution.

1. Stitch 2 rectangles together.

2. Stitch a rectangle to bottom left side of piece from Step 1.

3. Stitch a rectangle to bottom right side of piece from Step 2.

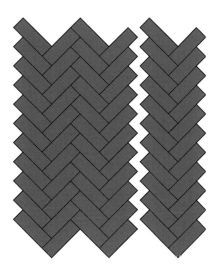

4. Continue adding rectangles to make a 2 × 11 column. Make 3 columns.

5. Arrange columns as shown. Join columns; see the *Great Assembly Tips*, page 94.

6. Mark a centered 11¾″ square on assembled block. Stay-stitch just outside the marked line (seam line). Trim away excess fabric outside seam line, leaving ¼″ seam allowance.

FINISHED BLOCK

GREAT PIECING TIPS

Use a window template or transparent ruler as a guide to mark stitching lines on all rectangles. All seam lines should be marked before stitching.

Mark, press, and handle your project carefully (and as little as possible) until the first border is added, to prevent the bias edges of the block from stretching before they are stitched to the straight-grain edges of the border. Do not slide the iron; lift and replace it.

Stitching the seam that joins two columns of chevrons involves sewing many inside corners; it is important to stitch exactly on the seam lines and not into the seam allowance. To assemble the quilt you will be stitching a series of short seams along the zigzag edges of the columns, which you might find easier to do by hand than by machine; secure the ends of each seam with backstitching.

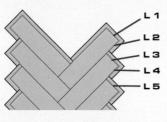

LEFT COLUMN

RIGHT COLUMN

1. Place left chevron column over right column as shown, aligning seam lines L1 and R1. Stitch L1/R1; finger press.

2. With left column still on top, align seam lines L2 and R2, rotating layers as shown. Stitch L2/R2; finger press.

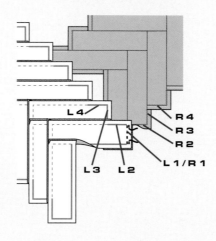

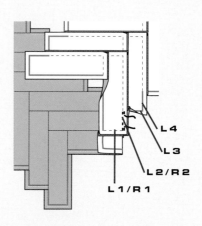

3. Continue stitching seam lines in sequential order.

4. Press the seam allowance after each short seam is stitched or wait until each zigzag seam has been stitched along its entire length. Press seam allowances as shown.

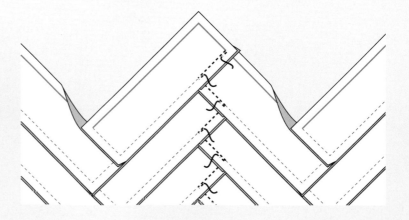

Borders

Join borders to quilt, first short strips at sides, then long strips at top and bottom. Complete first border before proceeding to second.

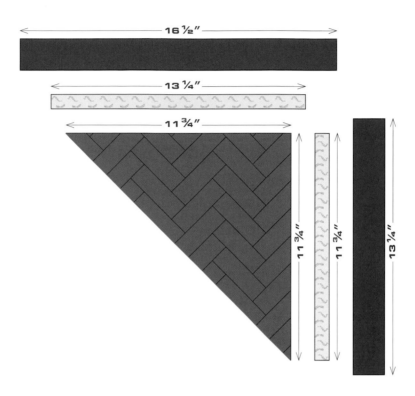

Finishing

1. Mark quilting designs on quilt top.

◆ *For second border:* Use a transparent ruler or template to mark an unbroken line of 1"-wide on-point squares so that there are 16 squares on each border side.

2. Prepare batting and backing.

3. Assemble quilt layers.

4. Quilt in-the-ditch on inner and outer border seams, and along zigzag seams connecting 1 × 11 halves of each 2 × 11 column. Quilt on all marked lines.

5. Trim batting and backing to ½" beyond outermost seam line.

6. Bind quilt edges.

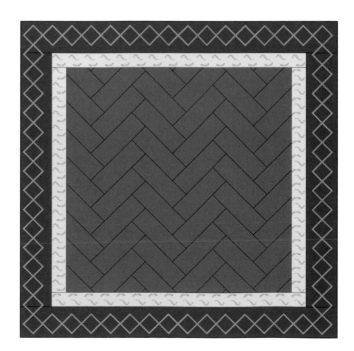

You can plan a Chevron block to be almost any size by changing the size and/or number of the components.

◆ The rectangular patches can be enlarged to almost any size, but should be reduced to no smaller than ½″; changing the height/width ratio of the rectangle's sides will also alter the appearance of the chevrons.

◆ To lengthen your project, add more pairs of rectangles to each column. To widen it, add more columns.

◆ Note that it is also possible to join columns of different-sized chevrons. Cut all the rectangles from strips of the same width, but make the length different for one or more columns. The longer the rectangles are in proportion to their width, the wider the column will be.

On this 84" x 94" antique quilt top, the rectangles are 1 ¾" x 6 ¼" and there are nine 2 x 36 columns.

This pattern is sometimes known as Coarse Woven, and it is filled with zigzags and columns; the way you place color in it will change its appearance as much as the palette you use. Whether you work in jewel tones or pastels, prints, stripes, or solids, consider using a contrasting element to trace a path over your quilt's surface.

Wholecloth Doll Quilt

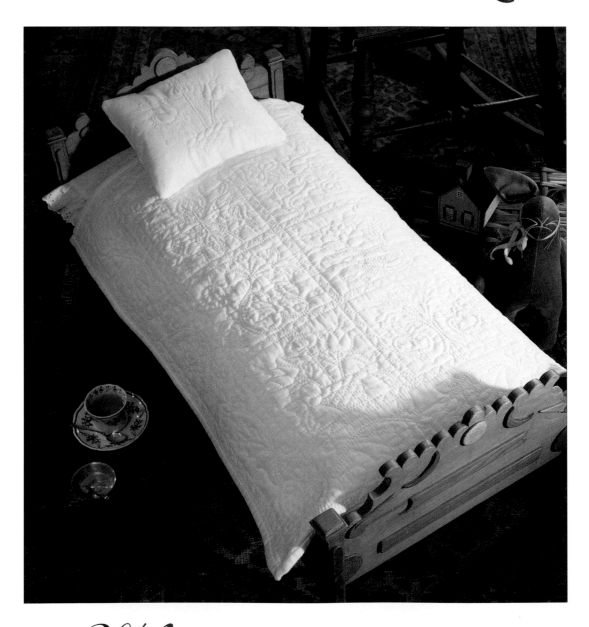

*W*hat quilter does not aspire to someday stitching a spectacular white-on-white quilt? Here is one small enough to complete in a busy lifetime. The patterns can be resized with a photocopier if you wish, worked together as a wholecloth quilt, or used individually to quilt blocks, sashing or borders wherever you like. We used trapunto to add extra relief to the doll quilt; turn to page 106 to see the effect when contrasting thread or pearl cotton is used.

THE COMPONENTS

Note: In the following directions the components are defined by lines of quilting rather than by seams. Dimensions for the quilt top are finished size.

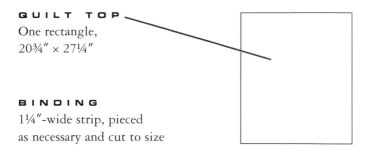

QUILT TOP
One rectangle,
20¾" × 27¼"

BINDING
1¼"-wide strip, pieced
as necessary and cut to size

FABRIC AND CUTTING LIST

Yardages are based on 44"-wide fabric; see the *Great Fabric Tips* on page 105. Cut rectangles following chart. Cut binding as directed below. All dimensions include ¼" seam allowance and binding includes extra length.

DIMENSIONS

FINISHED QUILT
20¾" × 27¼"

MATERIALS

☐ **WHITE SOLID**
2 yds. tightly woven fabric
(for quilt top, backing* and
binding)

☐ **WHITE SOLID**
¾ yd. loosely woven fabric
(for lining trapunto)

BINDING
Use ¼ yd. tightly woven white
solid to cut and piece a 1¼" ×
110" strip.

BATTING＊

THREAD
Sewing, quilting, embroidery

YARN/CORD
Cotton yarn/cord, ⅛" diameter

POLYESTER FIBERFILL
Loose fiberfill, for trapunto

*Backing and batting should be cut and
pieced as necessary so they are at least 4"
larger than quilt top on all sides, then
trimmed to size after quilting.

Fabric and Yardage	Number of Pieces			Size
	For Quilt Top	For Backing	For Lining	
White Solid (tightly woven) 1¾ yd.	1	—	—	21¼" × 27¾"
	—	1	—	29" × 36" (includes extra length and width)
White Solid (loosely woven) ¾ yd.	—	—	1	21¼" × 27¾"

Marking the Quilting Designs

On this project the seams between components (blocks, sashing, and borders) are simulated by straight lines of quilting around individual quilting designs. Each round dot on patterns and diagrams represents a French knot, which is embroidered after trapunto and conventional quilting are complete.

Mark design lines on quilt top as directed below. Use actual-size motif patterns on pages 108 to 113; do not re-mark straight outlines, which are given for positioning only.

1. Mark outer edge of second border ⅜″ inside seam line of quilt top, outlining a 20½″ × 27″ design area, centered. (Subsequent diagrams do not show fabric that extends beyond this design area.)

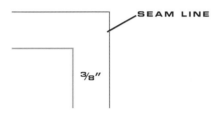

2. Mark additional outlines for blocks, sashing strips, and two borders as shown.

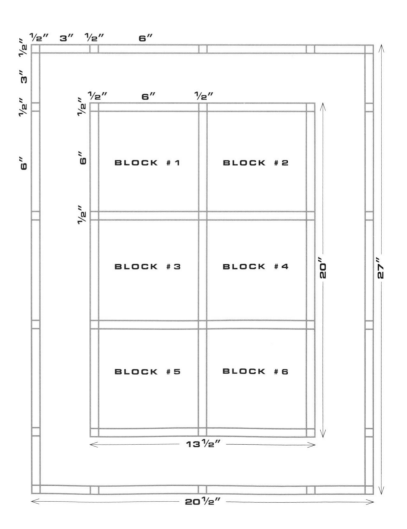

3. Mark floral motif on each block.

♦ *For Block #1:* Mark half-pattern on left half of block, centered between top and bottom edges; do not mark diamond grid on center flower yet. Reverse pattern to mark right half of block, then mark diamond grid on center flower.

♦ *For Blocks #2, #3, #4, and #5:* Mark pattern on each block, centered.

♦ *For Block #6:* Mark half-pattern on right half of block, centered between top and bottom edges. Reverse pattern to mark left half of block.

BLOCK #1

BLOCK #2

BLOCK #3

BLOCK #4

BLOCK #5

BLOCK #6

4. Mark geometric designs on sashing.

♦ *For sashing strips:* Mark a zigzag of 1″-long triangles on each strip.

♦ *For sashing squares:* Connect corners of each square to mark an ✕.

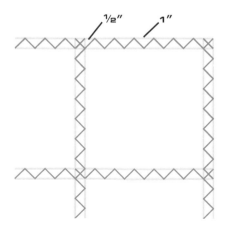

5. Mark motifs on first border, rotating quilt to mark each border side.

- *For each corner:* Mark heart and leaf at lower right, aligning center of heart with 45° diagonal center of corner. Reverse pattern, aligning on heart, to mark second leaf.

- *For each long side:* Mark grape cluster, centered between leaves and between inner and outer border edges.

6. Mark geometric designs on second border.

- Mark strips with zigzags of 1″-long triangles and border squares with X's in same manner as for sashing.

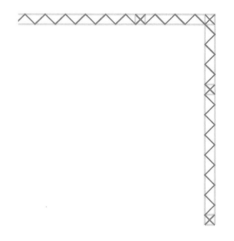

Trapunto

If you wish, add a trapunto relief to the quilt at this time; see *Working Trapunto,* opposite. Baste lining to back of quilt top. Hand-quilt motifs on blocks and first border that will be stuffed/corded for high relief; do not stitch single lines, such as small stems, tendrils, and zigzag grids, which will be quilted through a layer of batting in the traditional manner after stuffing. Stuff/cord the trapunto design areas.

In trapunto, parts of the quilting motifs are stuffed or corded to create high-relief designs. A loosely woven lining is placed behind the quilt top, with no batting between. Small closed areas of the motifs, such as leaves, stems, flower petals or the rim of a basket are outlined with quilting stitches and then filled with lengths of cotton yarn/cord and/or loose fiberfill that are inserted through the lining.

Preparing Quilt Top and Lining

1. Mark trapunto and traditional quilting designs on quilt top.
- *For stuffed designs:* Mark a single, closed outline for each shape to be stuffed.
- *For corded designs:* Mark double outlines to form channels slightly wider than diameter of yarn to be used, maintaining a uniform distance between pairs of parallel lines.

2. Cut lining same size as quilt top.
3. Pin lining to wrong side of quilt top, aligning edges; baste together as for traditional quilting but with 6″ to 8″ between columns and rows of basting stitches. Do not baste over trapunto designs. Machine-stitch ¼″ from edges.
4. Quilt by hand or machine on trapunto design lines.

Stuffing

1. Use appliqué scissors carefully to make a slit in lining at center of shape to be stuffed.

2. Working through slit, insert loose bits of fiberfill between quilt top and lining, using a blunt tool such as a crochet hook to distribute stuffing evenly.

3. Fill shape lightly but completely, checking front of quilt often. Do not overstuff.
4. Close slit with loose cross stitches or whipstitches.

Cording

1. Thread a long, blunt rug or tapestry needle with 15″ to 18″ length of yarn/cord.
2. Working through lining only, use tip of needle to make hole in channel large enough for needle to slip through.
3. Insert needle and slide it through channel between fabric layers as far as it can reach, then bring it out again on lining side. Pull cord until end disappears into needle entry point.

4. Reinsert needle at exit point and work it further along channel, then bring it up and re-enter channel as needed to cord its entire length.
- *To end a length of cord:* Bring needle out through lining and clip cord close to fabric, massaging the last needle exit point until end of cord disappears inside it.
- *To start a new length of cord:* Overlap end of previous length at least ½″ to prevent gaps in corded outline.

Prepare batting and backing. Assemble quilt layers. Hand-quilt on all marked lines not previously stitched, except round dots.

Embroidery

Use 2 or 3 strands of embroidery floss to stitch a French knot at each marked round dot on quilt top.

Finishing the Quilt

Trim batting and backing even with quilt top and lining. Bind quilt edges.

GREAT FABRIC TIPS

Although our designer chose white fabric for her quilt, you could make yours in any solid color. If you want to make a light color quilt top, use matching or white fabric for both the backing and lining; darker colors might show through as shadowing on the front.

To keep white or pale fabric from getting dirty while work is in progress, be sure your hands, work space, and tools are spotlessly clean and grease-free.

To avoid putting marks on your quilt, you can transfer the pattern for the quilting designs to tear-away interfacing or mark straight quilting lines with tape.

Instead of leaving your project out in the open when it isn't being worked on, place it folded (inside out) or flat into a pillowcase.

GREAT DESIGN IDEAS

You can make a small pillow to go with the doll quilt by centering and quilting one of the block motifs on a piece of matching fabric. The pillow in the photo is about 10″ wide and 7″ high and is finished with a plain knife edge. It is stuffed with fiberfill, but you could fill yours with balsam or potpourri instead.

Wholecloth Pillows

$\mathcal{T}$he Wholecloth Doll Quilt, page 98, was designed so that the motifs could be recombined to make other projects. The sashing and border motifs are proportioned so that they can be wrapped around a single block motif, or extended to fit around a layout that has any number of blocks. We made two pillows using the motifs from the middle blocks of the doll quilt. Each has the zigzag sashing and outer border along with part of the heart and leaf inner border. The lavender pillow is quilted with a slightly darker lavender thread, the white pillow with pretty shades of #8 pearl cotton. Because the designs are more visible with the contrasting stitching, neither was worked with trapunto.

Cut a 16½″ square of fabric for each pillow top and back. Make or purchase complementary cording; you will need about 2 yards.

Marking the Quilting Designs

Refer to the directions for the doll quilt to mark the designs on the pillow top.

1. Select one of the block motifs from the doll quilt. Center and mark it on the pillow top. Mark zigzag sashing and a matching outer border all around it.

2. Use the corner pattern on page 108 to mark a heart in each corner and one leaf on each side of the inner border.

Quilting

Layer pillow top, batting and lining. Quilt with thread to match your fabric, or use one or more contrasting colors of thread for a less formal look. Add French knots.

Finishing

After the quilting and embroidery are complete, add cording and a pillow back and insert a 16″-square knife-edge pillow form.

ACTUAL-SIZE
PATTERNS

LONG BORDER SIDE

BORDER
CORNER

BLOCK # 1

BLOCK # 6

BLOCK #2

BLOCK #3

BLOCK #4

BLOCK #5

Triangles-in-Triangles Runner

$\mathcal{T}$he traditional Economy Patch block, with the center composed of triangles, is the basis of this easy-to-make runner. Jean Hoblitzell, the designer of this extraordinary table runner, is also an architect. Her interest in light and space carries over to her quilted pieces. She often uses lightweight upholstery fabrics, chintz, and basketweave textures in her work, and suggests using sturdy interfacing rather than batting to fill a runner, so that it will be crisp and lie flat on the table.

Note: All dimensions are finished size.

CORNER TRIANGLE
4 corner triangles, 4″ on two sides,
5¾″ on third side

BLOCK
4 blocks, 5¾″ square

FIRST BORDER
4 strips, ½″ wide, cut to size
(top and bottom pieces added
before side pieces)

SETTING TRIANGLE
6 setting triangles, 5¾″ on two
sides, 8″ on third side

SECOND BORDER
4 strips, 2″ wide, cut to size

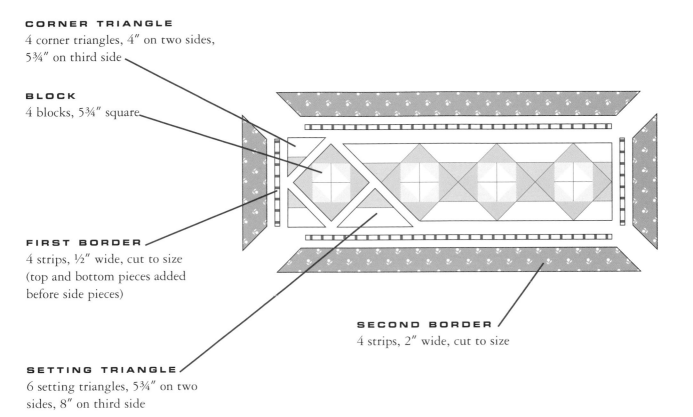

Yardages are based on 44″-wide fabric. Prepare templates, if desired, referring to drafting schematics. Cut strips and patches following schematics and chart. Except for drafting schematics, which give finished sizes, all dimensions include ¼″ seam allowance and strips include extra length, unless otherwise stated. (Note: Unmarked angles on cutting schematics are either 45° or 90°.)

DIMENSIONS

FINISHED BLOCK

5¾″ square, about 8⅛″ diagonal

FINISHED TABLE RUNNER

13″ × 37″

MATERIALS

- **ANTIQUE WHITE SOLID**
  ½ yd.

- **YELLOW SOLID**
  ¼ yd.

- **BLUE SOLID**
  ¼ yd.

- **GREEN SOLID**
  ¼ yd.

- **ORANGE-ON-WHITE PRINT**
  ¼ yd.

- **BLACK/WHITE STRIPED**
  ¼ yd.

- **BLUE FLORAL**
  ¼ yd.

- **BACKING** *
  1¼ yds.

- **BATTING** *

- **THREAD**

*Backing and batting should be cut and pieced as necessary so they are at least 4″ larger than quilt top on all sides, then trimmed to size after quilting.

DRAFTING SCHEMATICS

(No seam allowance added)

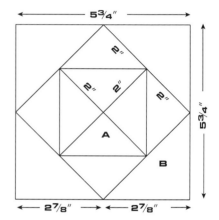

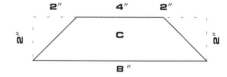

CUTTING SCHEMATICS

(Seam allowance included)

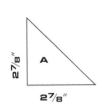

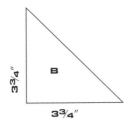

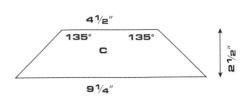

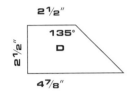

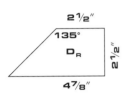

| Fabric and Yardage | FIRST CUT | | SECOND CUT | | | |
| | | | Number of Pieces | | | |
	Number of Pieces	Size	For 4 Blocks	For 6 Setting Triangles	For 4 Corner Triangles	Shape
PLAIN PATCHES						
Yellow Solid ¼ yd.	1	2⅞" × 40"	8	–	–	A
Orange-on-White Print ¼ yd.	1	2⅞" × 40"	8	–	–	A
Blue Solid ¼ yd.	1	2⅞" × 15"	–	–	4	A[1]
	1	6¼" × 40"	–	6	–	B[1]
Green Solid ¼ yd.	1	6¼" × 40"	16	–	–	B
Antique White Solid ½ yd.	2	2⅞" × 40"	–	–	4	A
	2	2½" × 40"	–	6	–	C
	1	2½" × 40"	–	–	2	D[2]
					2	D_R[2]
FIRST BORDER						
Black/White Striped ¼ yd.	2	1" × 20"				
	2	1" × 40"				
SECOND BORDER						
Blue Floral ¼ yd.	2	2½" × 20"				
	2	2½" × 40"				

[1] Cut blue A's from remainder of strip for B's.
[2] Cut D's and D_R's from same strip.

Block

Directions are given below for making one block. Amounts for making all 4 blocks at the same time are given in parentheses.

COLOR KEY
- ☐ Antique white solid
- ☐ Orange-on-white print
- ☐ Yellow solid
- ☐ Blue solid
- ☐ Green solid
- ☰ Black/white striped
- ▨ Blue floral

      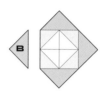

1. Join yellow and orange-on-white print A's in pairs to make 2 (8) A/A squares.

2. Join yellow and antique white A's in pairs to make 2 (8) A/A squares.

3. Join 4 A/A's to make one (4) center square.

4. Sew green B's to center square.

FINISHED BLOCK

Table Runner Center

1. Join C's and blue B's in pairs to make 6 setting triangles.

2. Join D's and blue A's in pairs to make 2 corner triangles.

3. Join D_R's and blue A's to make 2 reversed corner triangles.

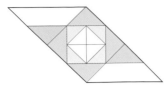
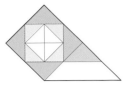

4. Sew one setting triangle each to 2 blocks.

5. Sew 2 setting triangles each to remaining 2 blocks.

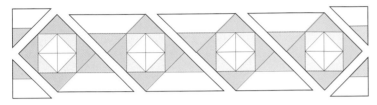

6. Arrange units as shown. Join units.

Borders

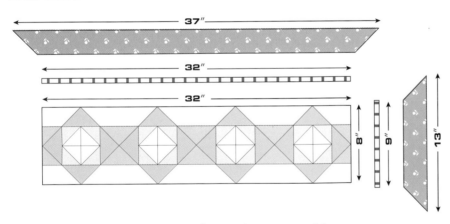

37"

32"

32"

8"

9"

13"

1. Join first border to quilt center, long strips at top and bottom, and then shorter strips at sides.

2. Join second border to first border, mitering corners.

Finishing

1. Prepare batting and backing.

2. Assemble quilt layers.

3. Quilt in-the-ditch on inner edge of first border and around blocks.

4. Bind quilt edges by pressing under edges of quilt top and backing, aligning folds and slipstitching together.

Notice how different parts of this pattern assume prominence or recede when the color values are differently arranged. Experiment with more or fewer colors, as suits your decor or dinnerware, or plan your runner to complement the season.

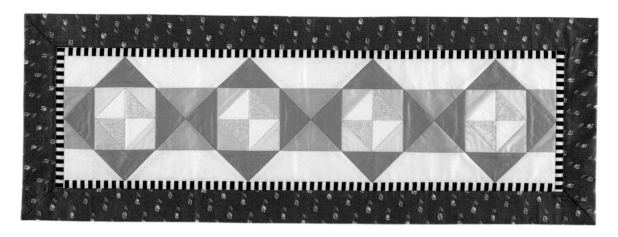

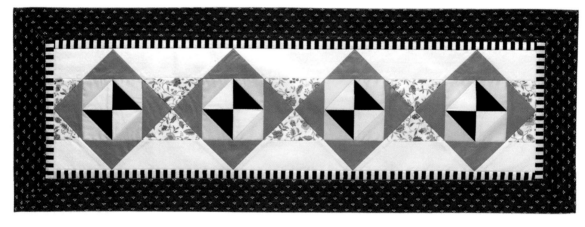

GREAT IDEAS

To make a very easy crib quilt or wallhanging, cut and piece 3 (or 4) strips of blocks, sew them together along the long edges, and then add borders. Your finished piece will be 37″ wide x 28″ long (or 37″ square).

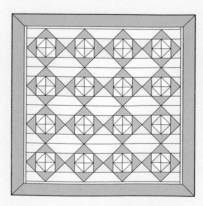

Photocopy this drawing, then create your own color scheme using colored pencils or markers.

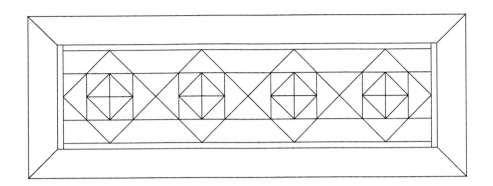

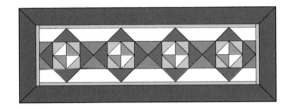

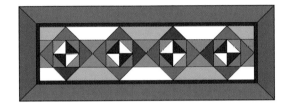

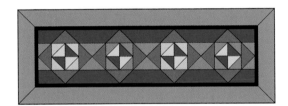

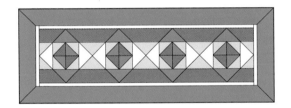

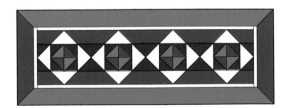

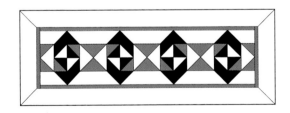

Dutchman's and Yankee Puzzle Quilt

$\mathcal{T}$his quilt was made to celebrate the marriage of a young American friend and the newlyweds' move to the Netherlands. Both of the quilt blocks have pinwheel centers; the Dutchman's Puzzle, made with large and small triangles, seems to have windmill blades, while the color arrangement of the Yankee Puzzle gives the appearance of a sawtooth border.

Note: All dimensions except for binding are finished size.
Amounts for full/queen are given in parentheses.

DUTCHMAN'S PUZZLE BLOCK
21 (45) blocks, 7″ square

PLAIN BLOCK
40 (84) blocks, 7″ square

YANKEE PUZZLE BLOCK
20 (40) blocks, 7″ square

FIRST BORDER
4 strips, 1¾″ wide, cut to size

SECOND BORDER
4 strips, ½″ wide, cut to size

THIRD BORDER
4 strips, 3½″ wide, cut to size

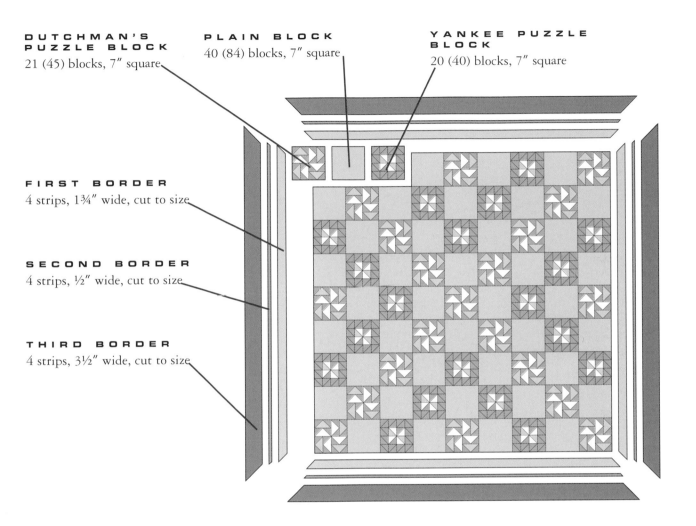

BINDING
1½″-wide strip, pieced as
necessary and cut to size

Note: Sizes and amounts for full/queen are given in parentheses.

Yardages are based on 44″-wide fabric. Prepare templates, if desired, referring to drafting schematics. Cut strips and patches following schematics and chart. Cut binding as directed below. Except for drafting schematics, which give finished sizes, all dimensions include ¼″ seam allowance and strips include extra length, unless otherwise stated. (Note: Angles on all patches are either 45° or 90°.)

DIMENSIONS

FINISHED BLOCK
7″ square, about 9⅞″ diagonal

FINISHED QUILT
73½″ (101″) square

MATERIALS

- **ANTIQUE WHITE PRINT**
  2½ (3¾) yds.

- **LT. GRAPE PRINT**
  5¾ (8¾) yds.

- **MED. GREEN PRINT**
  ¾ (1½) yds.

- **DK. GREEN PRINT**
  ¾ (1½) yds.

- **ROYAL BLUE PRINT**
  ¾ (1½) yds.

- **MED. GRAPE PRINT**
  1¼ (2¼) yds.

- **DK. GRAPE PRINT**
  ¾ (1½) yds.

- **DK. RED-PURPLE PRINT**
  3 (4) yds.

- **PURPLE FLORAL**
  2½ (3) yds.

- **BACKING** *
  5½ (9½) yds.

- **BATTING** *

- **THREAD**

- **BINDING**
  Use ½ yd. lt. grape print to make a 1½″ × 320″ (1½″ × 430″) strip.

*Backing and batting should be cut and pieced as necessary so they are at least 4″ larger than quilt top on all sides, then trimmed to size after quilting.

DRAFTING SCHEMATICS

(No seam allowance added)

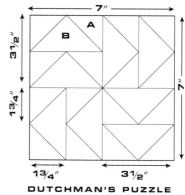

DUTCHMAN'S PUZZLE BLOCK

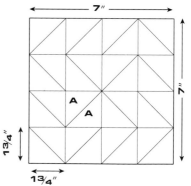

YANKEE PUZZLE BLOCK

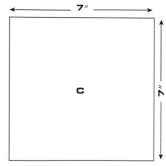

PLAIN BLOCK

CUTTING SCHEMATICS
(Seam allowance included)

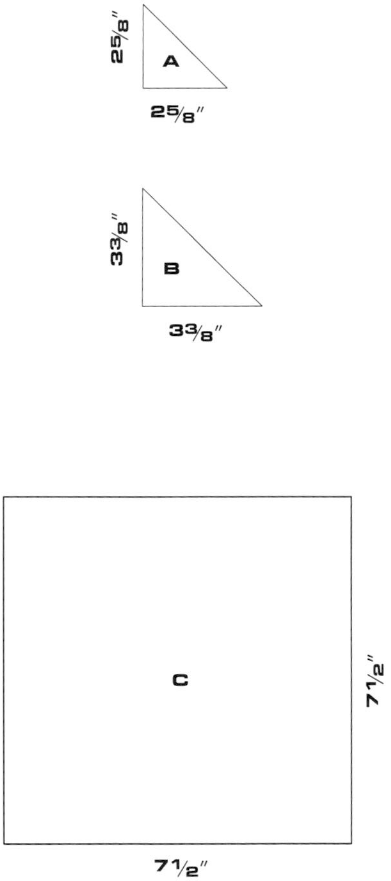

2⅝"

A

2⅝"

3⅜"

B

3⅜"

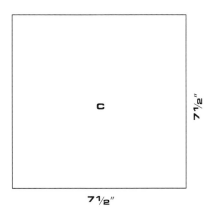

7½"

C

7½"

	FIRST CUT		SECOND CUT		
			Number of Pieces		
Fabric and Yardage	Number of Pieces	Size	For 40 (84) Plain Blocks	For 21 (45) Dutchman's Puzzle Blocks	Shape
PLAIN PATCHES					
Med. Green ¼ (½) yd.	2 (3)	2⅝" × 40"	–	42 (90)	A
Dk. Green ¼ (½) yd.	2 (3)	2⅝" × 40"	–	42 (90)	A
Royal Blue ¼ (½) yd.	2 (3)	2⅝" × 40"	–	42 (90)	A
Med. Grape ¼ (½) yd.	2 (3)	2⅝" × 40"	–	42 (90)	A
Dk. Grape ¼ (½) yd.	2 (3)	2⅝" × 40"	–	42 (90)	A
Red-Purple[1] 2¼ (3) yds.	1 (2)	2⅝" × 80"	–	42 (90)	A
SECOND BORDER					
	4	1⅞" × 78" (1⅞" × 106")			
Antique White ½ (1) yd.	4 (9)	3⅜" × 40"	–	84 (180)	B
Lt. Grape 4½ (7) yds.	2 (5)	3⅜" × 80"	–	84 (180)	B
	8 (17)	7½" × 40"	40 (84)	–	C
FIRST BORDER					
	4	2¼" × 77" (2¼" × 105")			
THIRD BORDER					
Purple Floral 2½ (3) yds.	4	4" × 84" (4" × 106")			

[1] Reserve remainder of fabric for cutting triangle squares.

	FIRST CUT		SECOND CUT	
Fabric and Yardage	Number of Pieces	Size	Number of Pieces For 20 (40) Yankee Puzzle Blocks	Shape
SPEEDY TRIANGLE SQUARES [1]				
Antique White and Lt. Grape ¾ (1¼) yd. each	2 (4)	8⅞″ × 19⅜″	40 (80)	A/A[2]
Antique White and Med. Grape ½ (¾) yd. each	1 (2)	8⅞″ × 19⅜″	20 (40)	A/A[3]
Antique White and Red-Purple ½ (¾) yd. each	1 (2)	8⅞″ × 19⅜″	20 (40)	A/A[4]
Assorted Green/ Blue/Grape Prints ½ (1) yd. each	6 (12)	14¾″ × 19⅜″	480 (960)	A/A[5]

[1] See *Speedy Triangle Squares* on page 221.
[2] Mark 3 × 7 grids with 2⅝″ squares.
[3] Mark 3 × 7 grids with 2⅝″ squares.
[4] Mark 3 × 7 grids with 2⅝″ squares. Use remainder of red-purple from border strips and plain patches.
[5] Mark 6 × 7 grids with 2⅝″ squares. Use 6 (12) different medium/dark combinations.

ADJUSTING THE SIZE

This quilt can be enlarged from twin to full/queen by increasing the number of blocks to make two additional rows on each side, continuing the overall pattern formed by the blocks, and increasing the length of the border strips to fit. Refer to the cutting charts, preceding page and above, for the number of pieces to cut for the different sizes.

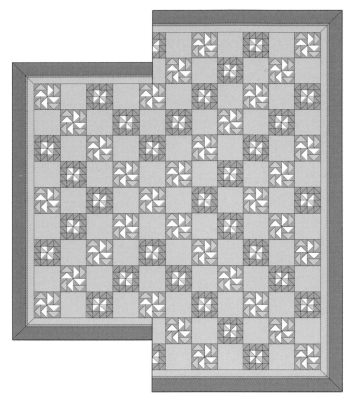

TWIN
40 plain blocks, 21 Dutchman's Puzzle blocks, 20 Yankee Puzzle blocks, quilt center 63″ square

FULL/QUEEN
84 plain blocks, 45 Dutchman's Puzzle blocks, 40 Yankee Puzzle blocks, quilt center 91″ square

---

BLOCK ASSEMBLY

Dutchman's Puzzle Block

Directions are given below for making one whole block. Amounts for making all 21 (twin) or 45 (full/queen) whole blocks at the same time are given in parentheses.

COLOR KEY
☐ Antique white print
☐ Lt. grape print
☐ Assorted green/blue/grape prints
☐ Purple floral

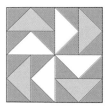

1. Sew 2 different assorted A's to each B to make 4 (84) (180) white/assorted and 4 (84) (180) lt. grape/assorted rectangles.

2. Join rectangles in pairs to make 4 (84) (180) quarter-blocks.

3. Arrange quarter-blocks as shown. Join quarter-blocks.

FINISHED DUTCHMAN'S PUZZLE BLOCK

Yankee Puzzle Block

Arrange A/A squares as shown to make 4 rows.
Join rows.

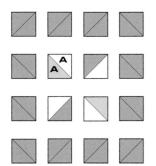

FINISHED YANKEE
PUZZLE BLOCK

Quilt Center

Arrange units as shown. Join units to make rows.
Join rows.

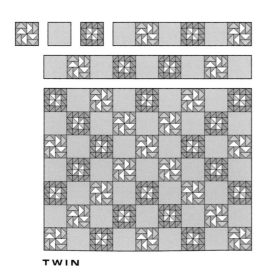

TWIN

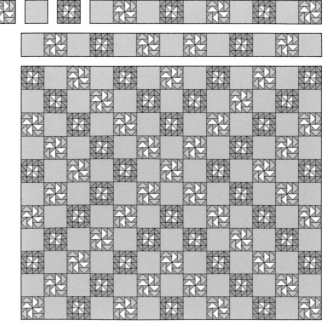

FULL/QUEEN

128

Borders

Join borders to quilt center, mitering corners.

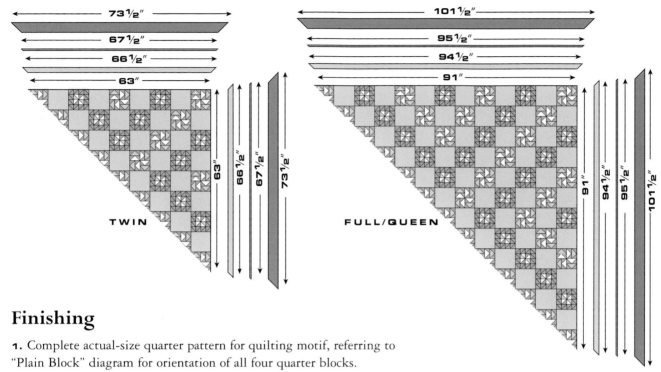

TWIN

FULL/QUEEN

Finishing

1. Complete actual-size quarter pattern for quilting motif, referring to "Plain Block" diagram for orientation of all four quarter blocks.

2. Mark quilting motif on each plain block.

3. Prepare batting and backing.

4. Assemble quilt layers.

5. Quilt plain blocks on marked lines and ¼″ inside seam lines. Quilt in-the-ditch on all seams of pieced blocks and on inner and outer seams of second border.

6. Trim batting and backing to ½″ beyond outermost seam line.

7. Bind quilt edges.

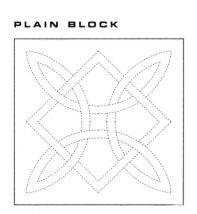

PLAIN BLOCK

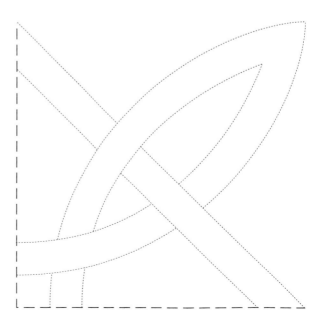

ACTUAL-SIZE QUARTER-PATTERN FOR QUILTING MOTIF

A change of color can give the Dutchman's and Yankee Puzzle a completely different feeling. You might want to use colors with more contrast, or make the two blocks very different from one another. You might also consider shading the color values from the center of the quilt out, or from one corner to another, to emphasize the diagonal arrangement of the blocks.

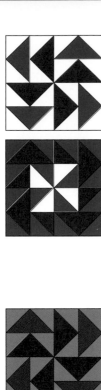

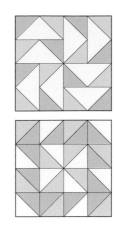

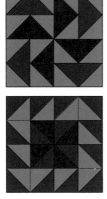
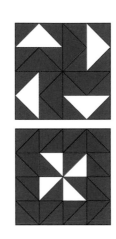
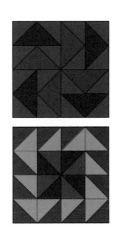

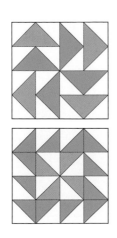
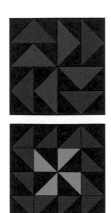
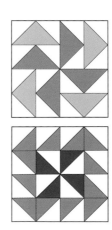

131

Photocopy this page, then create your own color scheme using colored pencils or markers. Refer to the examples on the previous pages, or design a unique color arrangement to match your decor or please your fancy.

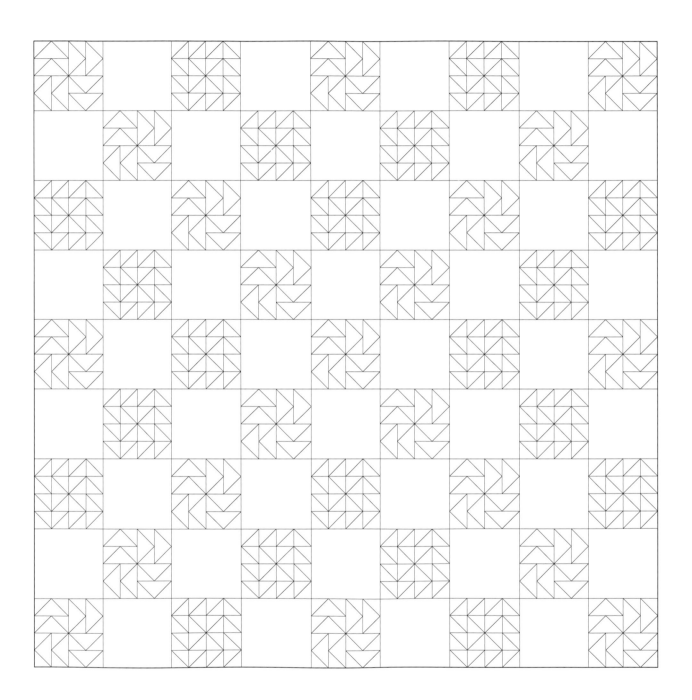

If you vary the setting angle from straight to diagonal, use or omit setting squares, or add sashing, you can create many intriguing allover patterns from the Dutchman's and Yankee Puzzle blocks. You can also use either of the blocks on its own. These variations may change the size of the quilt; you could compensate by using more or fewer blocks or borders. Diagonal sets may require half- or quarter-blocks.

Baskets Quilt

A bold sawtooth border gives a lively balance to this rendition of the always-popular basket pattern. The quilter of this antique piece attached her borders in a rather unusual and eccentric manner; we have given instructions for a more traditional and symmetrical arrangement.

Note: All dimensions except for binding are finished size.
Amounts for full/queen are given in parentheses.

BLOCK
13 blocks, 10″ square, with appliquéd handles

CORNER TRIANGLE
4 corner triangles, 7″ on two sides, about 10″ on third side

SETTING TRIANGLE
8 setting triangles, 10″ on two sides, about 14″ on third side

FIRST BORDER
4 pieced strips, 3½″-wide, plus four plain 3½″ corner squares

SECOND BORDER
4 pieced strips, 3½″-wide, plus four plain 3½″ corner squares

THIRD BORDER
4 pieced strips, 3½″-wide, plus four plain 3½″ corner squares

FOURTH BORDER
2 (4) pieced strips, 3½″-wide (plus four plain 3½″ corner squares)

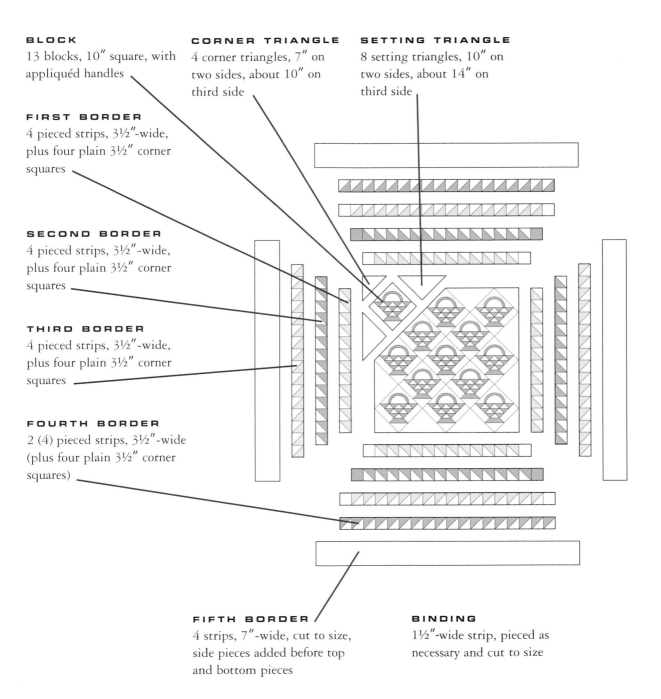

FIFTH BORDER
4 strips, 7″-wide, cut to size, side pieces added before top and bottom pieces

BINDING
1½″-wide strip, pieced as necessary and cut to size

Note: Sizes and amounts for full/queen are given in parentheses.

Yardages are based on 44″-wide fabric. Prepare templates, if desired, referring to drafting schematics. Cut strips and patches following schematics and chart. Cut binding and basket handles as directed below. Except for drafting schematics, which give finished sizes, all dimensions include ¼″ seam allowance. Except for basket handles, all strips include extra length, unless otherwise stated.

(Note: Unmarked angles on cutting schematics are either 45° or 90°.)

DIMENSIONS

FINISHED BLOCK
10″ square, about 14⅛″ diagonal

FINISHED QUILT
77″ × 84″ (84″ square)

MATERIALS

- **MUSLIN SOLID**
  9 (9½) yds.

- **BLUE DOTTED**
  1½ yds.

- **BROWN STRIPED**
  3½ (4) yds.

- **BACKING** *
  5 (5½) yds.

- **BATTING** *

- **THREAD**

- **BINDING**
  Use ½ yd. muslin solid to make a 1½″ × 340″ (1½″ × 360″) strip.

- **BASKET HANDLES**
  Use ½ yd. brown striped to cut 13 bias strips for appliqué, 1¾″ × 20½″.

*Backing and batting should be cut and pieced as necessary so they are at least 4″ larger than quilt top on all sides, then trimmed to size after quilting.

DRAFTING SCHEMATICS

(No seam allowance added)

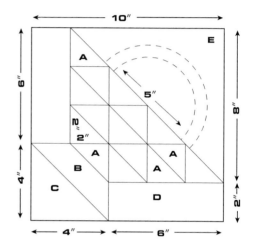

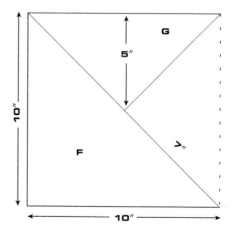

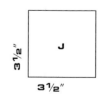

FIRST CUT			SECOND CUT						
			Number of Pieces						
Fabric and Yardage	Number of Pieces	Size	For 13 Blocks	For 8 Setting and 4 Corner Blocks	For First Border	For Second Border	For Third Border	For Fourth Border	Shape
PLAIN PATCHES									
Brown Striped ½ yd.	2	2⅞" × 40"	52	–	–	–	–	–	A
	1	4" × 40"	–	–	–	4	–	(4)	J
Muslin Solid 4¾ yds.	2	2½" × 100"	28	–	–	–	–	–	D
	2	8⅞" × 40"	13	–	–	–	–	–	E
	2	10⅞" × 40"	–	8	–	–	–	–	F
	1	7 9/16" × 18"	–	4	–	–	–	–	G
	1	4" × 40"	–	–	4	–	4	–	J
FIFTH BORDER									
	2	7½" × 80"							
	2	7½" × 87" (4½" × 94")							

FIRST CUT			SECOND CUT					
			Number of Pieces					
Fabric and Yardage	Number of Pieces	Size	For 13 Blocks	For First Border	For Second Border	For Third Border	For Fourth Border	Shape
SPEEDY TRIANGLE SQUARES[1]								
Brown Striped and Muslin Solid 1¼ (1¾) yds. each	1	15⅜" × 21⅛"	65	–	–	–	–	A/A[2]
	3 (4)	18½" sq.	–	–	56	–	36 (72)	H/H[3]
Blue dotted and Muslin Solid 1¼ yds. each	4	18½" sq.	–	48	–	64	–	H/H[3]
STRIP-PIECED BIAS SQUARES[4]								
Muslin Solid and Brown Striped 1 yd. each	2	2 1/16" × 40"						A/B/C
	2	1 15/16" × 40"						
	2	3½" × 40"						

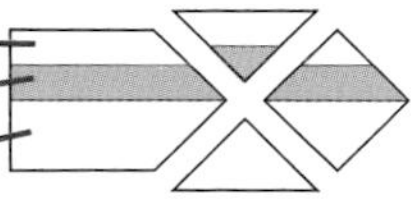

[1] See *Speedy Triangle Squares* on page 221.
[2] Mark 5 × 7 grids of 2⅞" squares.
[3] Mark 4 × 4 grids of 4⅜" squares.
[4] Cut strips on the bias and join lengthwise with brown striped between muslin solid strips as shown. Cut 13 A/B/C squares.

CUTTING SCHEMATICS

(Seam allowance included)

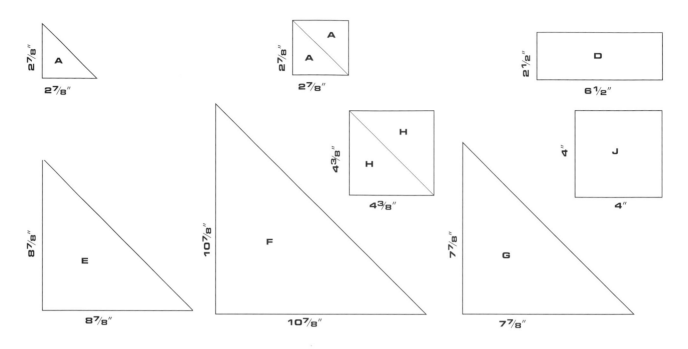

ADJUSTING THE SIZE

This quilt can be enlarged easily from twin to full/queen by adjusting the fourth and fifth borders. For the fourth (pieced) border, add plain corner squares to the ends of the top and bottom strips and make two strips for the sides. For the fifth (plain) border, increase the length of the strips to fit.

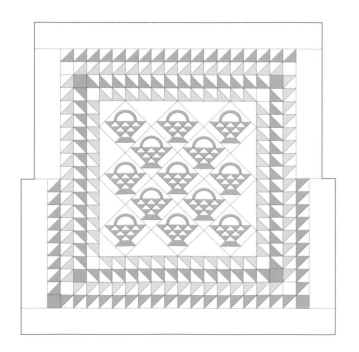

TWIN
3 pieced strips at sides,
4 pieced strips at top
and bottom

FULL/QUEEN
4 pieced strips on all sides

Block

Directions are given below for making one block. Amounts for making all 13 blocks at the same time are given in parentheses.

COLOR KEY
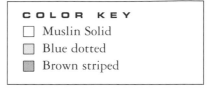
☐ Muslin Solid
☐ Blue dotted
◼ Brown striped

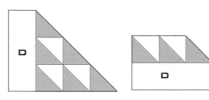

1. Sew together an A and an A/A square to make one (13) short strip.

2. Sew together an A and two A/A squares to make 2 (26) long strips.

3. Arrange pieced and plain units as shown to make 3 rows. Join rows.

4. Join one D to piece from Step 3 and another to remaining long strip.

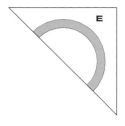

5. Press under ¼″ on long edges of bias strip for handle. Curve strip into a semicircle and appliqué it on E.

6. Arrange units as shown. Join units.

FINISHED BLOCK

Quilt Center

Arrange units as shown. Join units to make rows. Join rows.

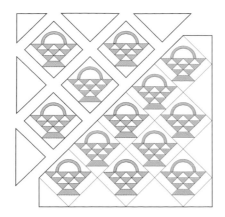

Borders

Varying amounts and directions for full/queen are given in parentheses. Refer to diagrams for orientation of triangle squares in sawtooth strips on all sides of quilt. (Left- and right-side strips are identical; top and bottom strips are identical and the opposite of side strips. Refer to the "Components" diagram on page 135 as well.)

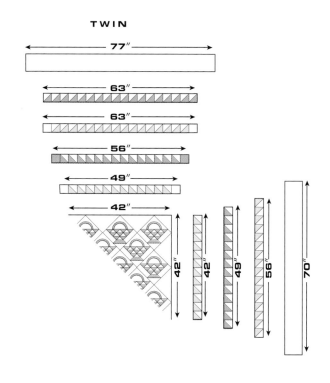

TWIN

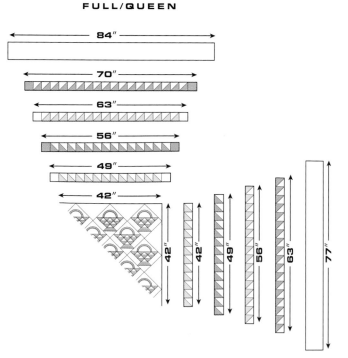

FULL/QUEEN

1. For first border, join 12 blue/muslin H/H squares to make 4 sawtooth strips. Sew a muslin J to ends of top and bottom strips.

2. For second border, join 14 brown/muslin H/H squares to make 4 sawtooth strips. Sew a brown J to ends of top and bottom strips.

3. For third border, join 16 blue/muslin H/H squares to make 4 sawtooth strips. Sew a muslin J to ends of top and bottom strips.

4. For fourth border, join 18 brown/muslin H/H squares to make 2 (4) sawtooth strips. (Sew a brown J to ends of top and bottom strips.)

5. Join first, second, and third borders to quilt center, short strips at sides, then longer strips at top and bottom.

6. Join fourth border to quilt top and bottom. (Join short strips to quilt sides, then longer strips to quilt top and bottom.)

7. Join fifth border to quilt, short strips at sides, then longer strips at top and bottom.

Finishing

Amounts for full/queen are given in parentheses.

1. Mark quilting designs on quilt top: Mark lines for single-outline, double-outline, echo, and allover quilting ½″ from seams and/or ½″ apart. Mark 1½″ semi-circles under basket handle. For plain and pieced border squares, mark 2½″ circles. For plain border, mark echoing diamonds, starting at center of each quilt side and working outward to ends; mark 20 diamonds on quilt sides; mark 22 (24) on top and bottom.

2. Prepare batting and backing.

3. Assemble quilt layers.

4. Quilt on marked lines.

5. Trim batting and backing to ½″ beyond outermost seam line.

6. Bind quilt edges.

BASKET BLOCK

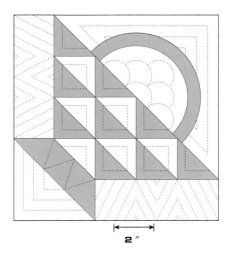

2″

BORDER SQUARE

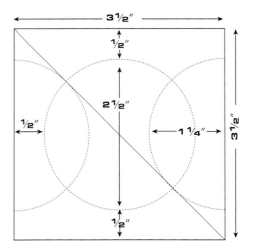

3½″
½″
2½″
½″
1¼″
½″
3½″

SETTING TRIANGLE

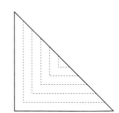

CORNER TRIANGLE

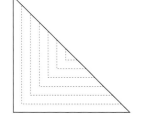

PLAIN BORDER

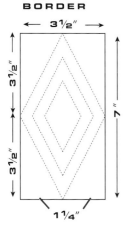

3½″
3½″
3½″
7″
1¼″

TWIN

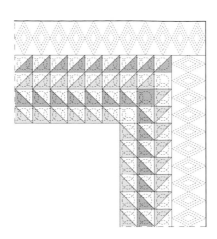

FULL/QUEEN

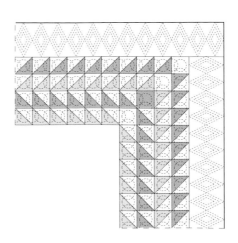

Pinwheel Star Quilt

Motion on a grand scale here, as giant stars spin in a blur of red and white and blue. Your focus shifts from the red to the white and back again, while the border width holds the movement in perfect balance. Each block mixes squares and triangles; when set together, alternate rows of white and red stars appear. This dynamic pattern is easy to reproduce as shown, or play with color placement in the block and see other intriguing patterns emerge.

Note: All dimensions are finished size.
Amounts for full/queen are given in parentheses.

BLOCK
36 (64) blocks, 10″ square

FIRST BORDER
4 strips, 2½″ wide,
cut to size

SECOND BORDER
4 strips, 2½″ wide,
cut to size

THIRD BORDER
4 strips, 2½″ wide,
cut to size

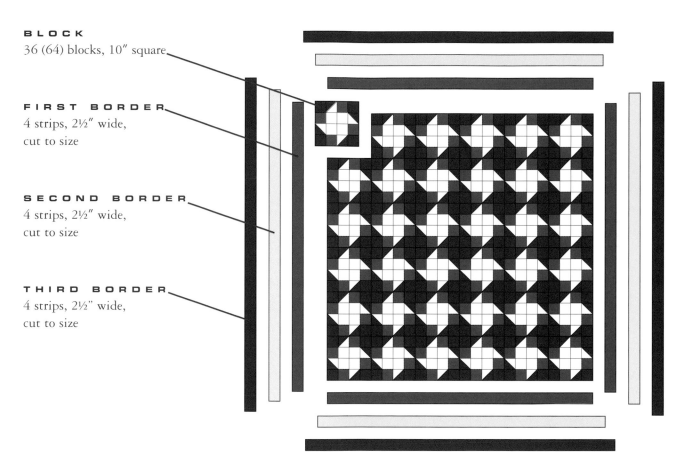

GREAT SIZING TIPS

Because this pattern will repeat continuously no matter how many blocks are placed in each row or column, you can plan your quilt to be almost any size you wish. Just remember that the length of each edge will be a multiple of 10″ (one block) plus 15″ (the width of the borders).

4 blocks in a 2 x 2 layout = 35″-square wallhanging
9 blocks in a 3 x 3 layout = 45″-square wallhanging
15 blocks in a 3 x 5 layout = 45″ x 65″ crib quilt

Note: Sizes and amounts for full/queen are given in parentheses.

Yardages are based on 44″-wide fabric. Prepare templates, if desired, referring to drafting schematics. Cut strips and patches following schematics and chart. Except for drafting schematics, which give finished sizes, all dimensions include ¼″ seam allowance and strips include extra length, unless otherwise stated. (Note: Angles on all patches are either 45° or 90°.)

DIMENSIONS

FINISHED BLOCK
10″ square; about 14½″ diagonal

FINISHED QUILT
75″ (95″) square

MATERIALS

☐ **WHITE SOLID**
2¾ (3½) yds.

☐ **MUSLIN SOLID**
2½ (3) yds.

■ **RED SOLID**
4 (5) yds.

■ **BLUE SOLID**
2½ (3) yds.

BACKING *
5 (9) yds.

BATTING *

THREAD

QUILTING TEMPLATE
2-line cable, 2″ high

*Backing and batting should be cut and pieced as necessary so they are at least 4″ larger than quilt top on all sides, then trimmed to size after quilting.

DRAFTING SCHEMATICS
(No seam allowance added)

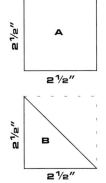

CUTTING SCHEMATICS
(Seam allowance included)

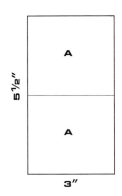

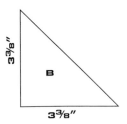

FIRST CUT			SECOND CUT	
Fabric and Yardage	Number of Pieces	Size	Number of Pieces For 36 (64) Blocks	Shape
PLAIN PATCHES				
White Solid 1¼ (1¾) yd.	12 (20)	3″ × 40″	144 (256)	A
SPEEDY TRIANGLE SQUARES [1]				
White Solid 1¼ (1½) yds. and Red Solid[2]	2 (4)	21¼″ square	144 (256)	B/B
FIRST BORDER				
Blue Solid[3] 2½ (3) yds.	2	3″ × 70″ (3″ × 90″)		
	2	3″ × 75″ (3″ × 95″)		
SECOND BORDER				
Muslin Solid 2½ (3) yds.	2	3″ × 75″ (3″ × 95″)		
	2	3″ × 80″ (3″ × 100″)		
THIRD BORDER				
Red Solid[4] 2½ (3) yds.	2	3″ × 80″ (3″ × 100″)		
	2	3″ × 85″ (3″ × 105″)		

[1] See *Speedy Triangle Squares*, page 221. Mark 6 × 6 grids of 3⅜″ squares.
[2] Use remainder of red solid from third border.
[3] Reserve remainder of fabric for cutting strip-pieced patches.
[4] Reserve remainder of fabric for cutting triangle squares.

FIRST CUT			SECOND CUT		
Fabric and Yardage	Number of Pieces	Size	Method	Number of Pieces	Shape
STRIP-PIECED PATCHES [1]					
Red Solid 1¼ (1¾) yds. and Blue Solid[2]	12 (20)	3″ × 40″		144 (256)	A/A
	12 (20)	3″ × 40″			

[1] Join strips lengthwise.
[2] Use remainder of blue solid from first border.

The size of this coverlet can be adjusted easily from twin to full/queen if the number of blocks is increased to make two additional rows and columns. Refer to the cutting charts, page 145, for the number of pieces to cut for the different sizes; see also the *Great Sizing Tips*, page 143.

TWIN
36 blocks in
a 6 × 6 layout

FULL/QUEEN
64 blocks in
an 8 × 8 layout

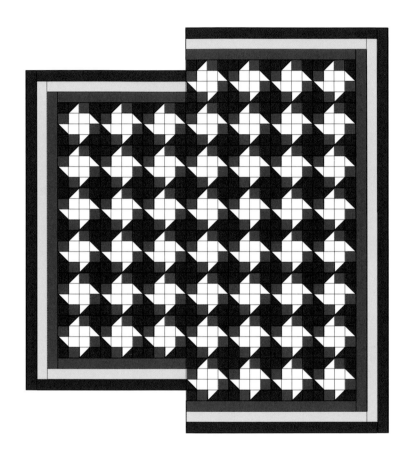

GREAT ACCESSORY IDEAS

You can add one 2½″ -wide border to a single block to make a 15″-square pillow front. You can also rearrange the quarter-blocks to form other interesting pinwheels.

To make a pillow, first assemble the layers and quilt the pillow front, then add a pillow back and stuff with either fiberfill or a 15″-square knife-edge pillow form.

 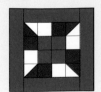 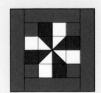

Block

Directions are given below for making one block. Amounts for making all 36 (twin) or 64 (full/queen) blocks at the same time are given in parentheses.

1. Join patches as shown to make 4 (144) (256) quarter-blocks.

2. Join 4 quarter-blocks, rotating as shown.

FINISHED BLOCK

Quilt Center

Arrange blocks as shown. Join blocks to make rows. Join rows.

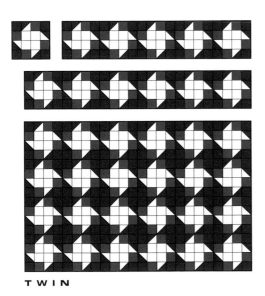

TWIN

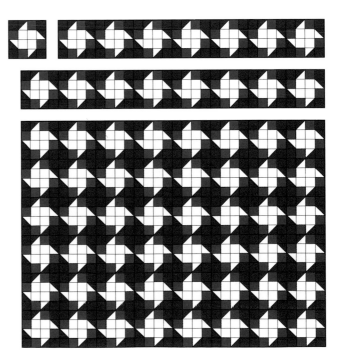

FULL/QUEEN

Borders

Join borders to quilt center, first shorter strips at top and bottom, then longer strips at sides. Complete first border before proceeding to second, then third.

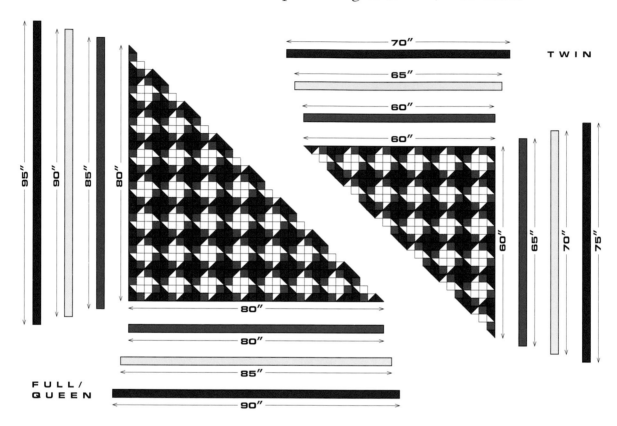

TWIN

FULL/QUEEN

Finishing

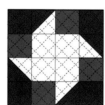

1. Mark quilting designs on quilt top.
- *For quilt center:* Mark an allover grid of 1″ squares, making lines parallel to diagonal seams. Do not mark seams.
- *For borders:* Use 2″-high 2-line cable template to mark a continuous design on each border strip, centering cables. Mark each border strip from the center outward, then mark identical symmetrical corners.

2. Prepare batting and backing.
3. Assemble quilt layers.
4. Quilt on all marked lines.
5. Trim batting even with outermost seam line. Trim quilt front and backing to ¼″ beyond batting. Bind quilt edges by pressing under ¼″ at edges of quilt top and backing, aligning folds, and slipstitching together.

A change of color can give the Pinwheel Star pattern a very different feeling. Jewel tones combined with black will make it dramatic, pastels will impart charm. Choosing prints will soften the overall pattern, while carefully cut stripes will emphasize it. Note how the pattern shifts when the placement of the colors varies from one part of the quilt to another.

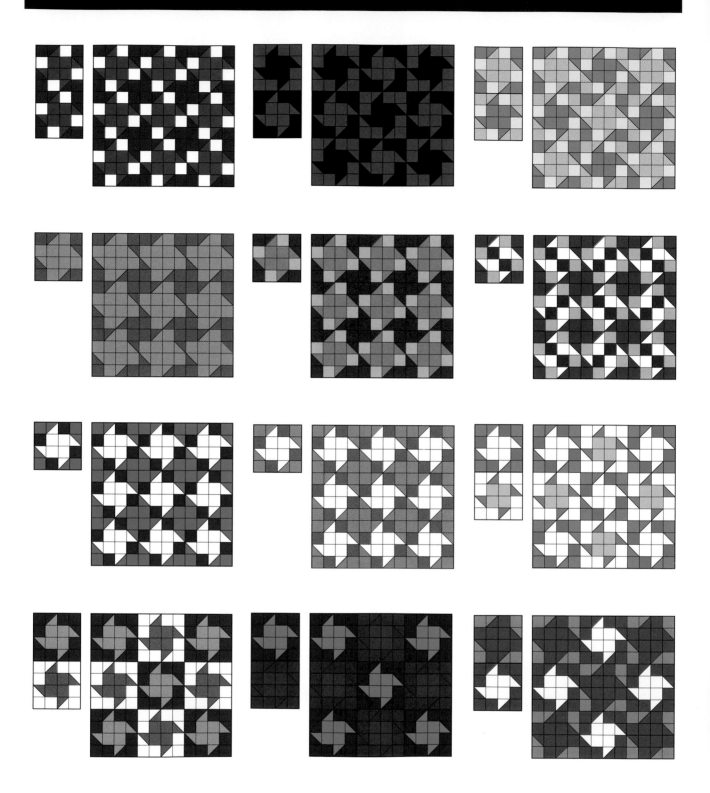

Country Patches Flag Quilt

$\mathcal{T}$he effect of this clever Nine-Patch and Triangle Square interpretation of the Stars and Stripes is that of a flag waving in the breeze on a hazy day. This charming—and very easy—project was designed using muted patriotic tones, but you can just as happily interpret it in clearer hues. Turn to page 158 to see how, by choosing other color values, or by arranging colors differently, you can transform this pattern in unexpected ways, creating a plaid or even a field of stylized Christmas trees.

Note: All dimensions except for binding are finished size.

NAVY TRIANGLE SQUARE BLOCK
4 blocks, 6″ square

BINDING
1″-wide strip, pieced as necessary and cut to size

NAVY 9-PATCH BLOCK
5 blocks, 6″ square

ECRU 9-PATCH BLOCK
11 blocks, 6″ square

ECRU TRIANGLE SQUARE BLOCK
13 blocks, 6″ square

RED 9-PATCH BLOCK
16 blocks, 6″ square

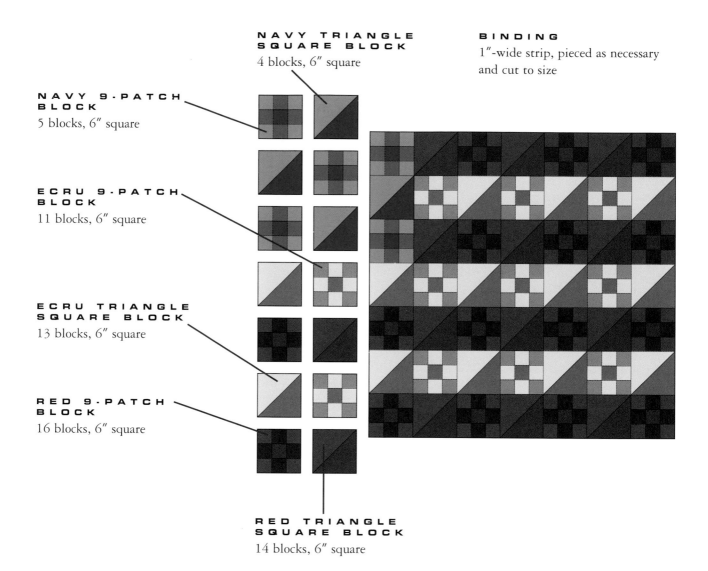

RED TRIANGLE SQUARE BLOCK
14 blocks, 6″ square

GREAT ACCESSORY IDEAS

You can make a Country Patches pillow or small wallhanging by reducing the finished size of the components. If you reduce the block pieces 50% (A = 1″ square; B/B = 3″ square), you will have a 27″ x 21″ quilt front.

For a pillow, assemble the layers, quilt them, add a pillow back, then stuff with fiberfill.

For a small wallhanging, assemble the quilt in the same manner as for the full-size wallhanging, or omit the binding and display the wallhanging in a frame.

Yardages are based on 44″-wide fabric. Prepare templates, if desired, referring to drafting schematics. Cut strips and patches following schematics and chart. Cut binding as directed below. Except for drafting schematics, which give finished sizes, all dimensions include ¼″ seam allowance and strips include extra length, unless otherwise stated. (Note: Angles on all patches are either 45° or 90°.)

DIMENSIONS

FINISHED 9-PATCH BLOCK
6″ square; about 8½″ diagonal

FINISHED TRIANGLE SQUARE BLOCK
6″ square; about 8½″ diagonal

FINISHED QUILT
54″ × 42″

MATERIALS

LT. PINK-ON-ECRU PRINT
½ yd.

LT. RED-ON-ECRU PRINT
½ yd.

MED. PINK-ON-ECRU PRINT
½ yd.

DK. PINK-ON-ECRU PRINT
¼ yd.

DK. RED-ON-ECRU PRINT
½ yd.

LT. RED/ECRU CHECK
½ yd.

MED. RED/ECRU CHECK
½ yd.

MED. RED/GOLD PLAID
¼ yd.

DK. RED/GOLD STRIPE
½ yd.

DK. RED/GOLD PRINT
½ yd.

LT. NAVY/ECRU PLAID
¼ yd.

MED. NAVY/ECRU STRIPE
¼ yd.

MED. NAVY/ECRU CHECK
¼ yd.

DK. NAVY/ECRU PLAID
¼ yd.

DK. ECRU-ON-NAVY PRINT
¼ yd.

BINDING
½ yd. dk. navy/white stripe, cut and pieced to make a 1″ × 220″ bias strip.

BACKING *
3 yds.

BATTING *

THREAD

*Backing and batting should be cut and pieced as necessary so they are at least 4″ larger than quilt top on all sides, then trimmed to size after quilting.

FIRST CUT			SECOND CUT		
Fabric and Yardage	Number of Pieces	Size	Method	Number of Pieces	Shape
STRIP-PIECED ECRU PATCHES*					
Med. Pink Print ½ yd. and Lt. Pink Print ¼ yd.	4	2½" × 40"		22	A/A/A
	2	2½" × 40"			
Lt. Pink Print ½ yd. and Dk. Pink Print ¼ yd.	2	2½" × 40"		11	A/A/A
	1	2½" × 40"			
STRIP-PIECED RED PATCHES*					
Lt. Check and Dk. Print ¼ yd. each	4	2½" × 40"		32	A/A/A
	2	2½" × 40"			
Dk. Print and Med. Plaid ¼ yd. each	2	2½" × 40"		16	A/A/A
	1	2½" × 40"			
STRIP-PIECED NAVY PATCHES*					
Lt. Plaid and Med. Check ¼ yd. each	2	2½" × 40"		10	A/A/A
	1	2½" × 40"			
Med. Check and Dk. Print ¼ yd. each	2	2½" × 40"		5	A/A/A
	1	2½" × 40"			

* Join strips lengthwise, alternating colors as shown.

FIRST CUT			SECOND CUT	
Fabric and Yardage	Number of Pieces	Size	Number of Pieces	Shape
SPEEDY ECRU TRIANGLE SQUARES[1]				
Lt. Red Print and Dk. Red Print ½ yd. each	1	14¾" × 28½"	13	B/B[2]
SPEEDY RED TRIANGLE SQUARES[1]				
Med. Check and Dk. Stripe ½ yd. each	1	14¾" × 28½"	14	B/B[2]
SPEEDY NAVY TRIANGLE SQUARES[1]				
Med. Stripe and Dk. Plaid ¼ yd. each	1	7⅞" × 14¾"	4	B/B[3]

[1] See *Speedy Triangle Squares*, page 221.
[2] Mark 2 × 4 grid of 6⅞" squares.
[3] Mark 1 × 2 grid of 6⅞" squares.

DRAFTING SCHEMATICS
(No seam allowance added)

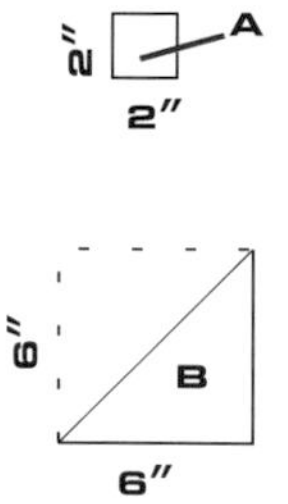

CUTTING SCHEMATICS
(Seam allowance included)

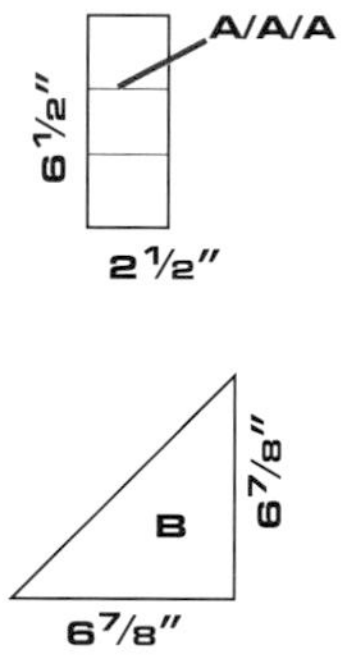

9-Patch Blocks

1. Join 3 ecru A/A/A strips as shown to make 11 blocks.

2. Join 3 red A/A/A strips as shown to make 16 blocks.

3. Join 3 navy A/A/A strips as shown to make 5 blocks.

QUILT ASSEMBLY

Quilt Center

1. Arrange navy blocks as shown, alternating 9-patches and triangle squares.

2. Join 3 red triangle squares and 3 red 9-patches to make 2 short strips.

3. Join 3 ecru 9-patches and 3 ecru triangle squares to make one short strip.

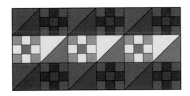

4. Join short strips, alternating colors and block types, to make a short striped field.

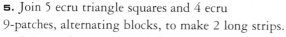

5. Join 5 ecru triangle squares and 4 ecru 9-patches, alternating blocks, to make 2 long strips.

6. Join 5 red 9-patches and 4 red triangle squares to make 2 long strips.

7. Join long strips, alternating colors and block types, to make a long striped field.

8. Arrange units as shown. Join units to make 2 rows. Join rows.

Finishing

1. Prepare batting and backing.

2. Assemble quilt layers.

3. Quilt in-the-ditch on all diagonal seams.

4. Trim batting and backing to ¼″ beyond outermost seam line.

5. Bind quilt edges.

GREAT SIZING TIPS

Because this pattern will repeat continuously no matter how many blocks are placed in each row or column, you can plan your quilt to be almost any size you wish. Just remember that the length of each edge will be a multiple of 6″ (one block). Note that not all configurations will work as flags. Note also, because this is a two-block pattern, that if each row and column of your layout contains an even number of blocks, the corner blocks will not be the same.

9 blocks in a 3 x 3 layout = 18″-square wallhanging

63 blocks in a 7 x 9 layout = 42″ x 54″ crib quilt (shown)

176 blocks in an 11 x 16 layout = 66″ x 96″ twin quilt

224 blocks in a 14 x 16 layout = 84″ x 96″ full/queen quilt

While the designer's clever arrangement of muted reds, whites and blues gives her
quilt the look of a flag waved by the wind, you can make this simple pattern in any palette you
like. It will look remarkably different if you use fewer colors, or fewer values of each color.
It would also be charming as a scrap quilt.

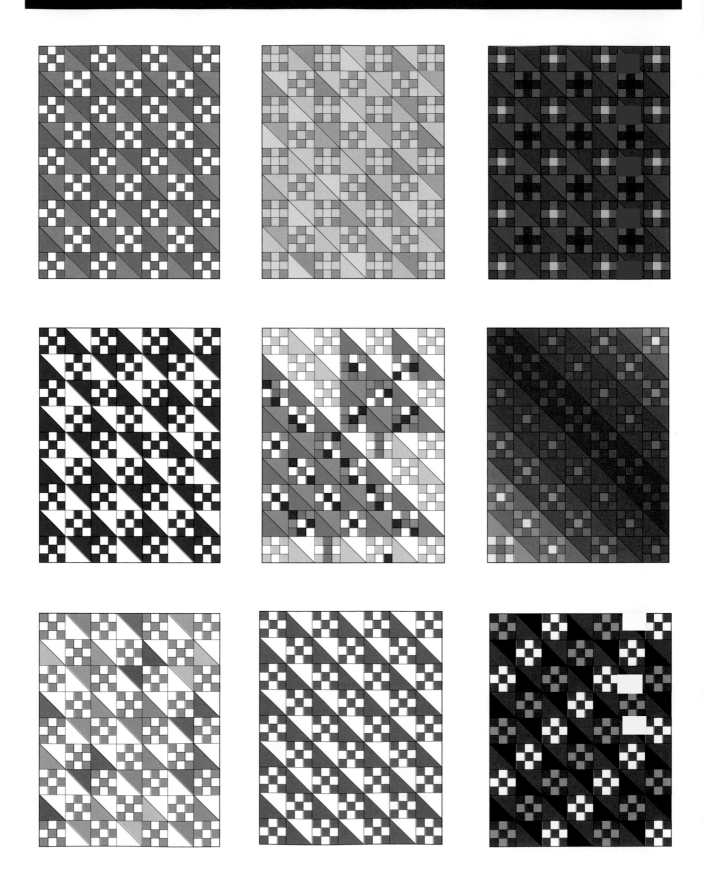

This quilt is made from two classic blocks, and you can, of course, use either one alone, set with sashing or plain setting squares, to make any number of familiar patterns. But you can also arrange the two blocks in other ways, and some of these can be made even more interesting with the addition of sashing.

Pine Burr Quilt

*J*ust one quilt block and two colors assembled in a positive/negative pattern make this easy-to-achieve quilt absolutely striking. Areas of light color seem to come forward, areas of dark color seem to recede, and different geometric configurations emerge as you adjust your focus. Interestingly, where the corners of four blocks come together, the pattern known as Old Maid's Ramble can be seen.

Note: All dimensions except for binding are finished size.
Amounts for full / queen are given in parentheses.

POSITIVE BLOCK
28 (45) blocks, 10″ square

NEGATIVE BLOCK
28 (45) blocks, 10″ square

BINDING
1½″-wide strip, pieced as
necessary and cut to size

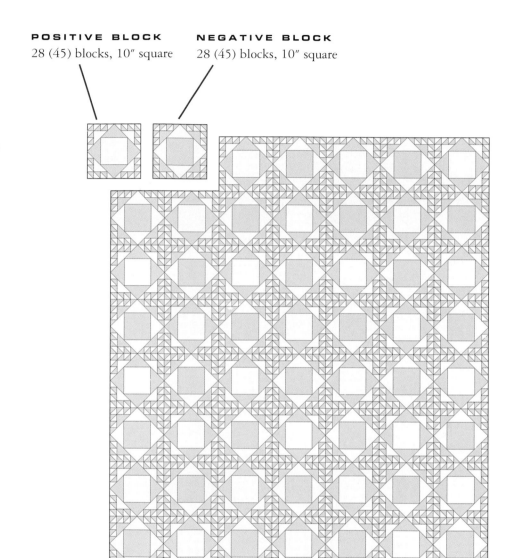

Note: Sizes and amounts for full/queen are given in parentheses.

Yardages are based on 44″-wide fabric. Prepare templates, if desired, referring to drafting schematic. Cut strips and patches following schematics and chart. Except for drafting schematic, which gives finished sizes, all dimensions include ¼″ seam allowance and strips include extra length, unless otherwise stated.
(Note: Angles on all patches in this project are either 45° or 90°.)

DIMENSIONS

FINISHED BLOCK
10″ square, about 14⅛″ diagonal

FINISHED QUILT
70″ × 80″ (90″ × 100″)

MATERIALS

- **YELLOW SOLID**
  6½ (8½) yds.

- **DK. GREEN SOLID**
  6½ (8½) yds.

- **BACKING** *
  5 (9) yds.

- **BATTING** *

- **THREAD**

- **BINDING**
  Use ½ yd. green solid to make a 1½″ × 340″ (1½″ × 420″) strip.

*Backing and batting should be cut and pieced as necessary so they are at least 4″ larger than quilt top on all sides, then trimmed to size after quilting.

DRAFTING SCHEMATIC

(No seam allowance added)

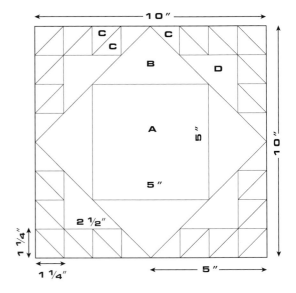

CUTTING SCHEMATICS
(Seam allowance included)

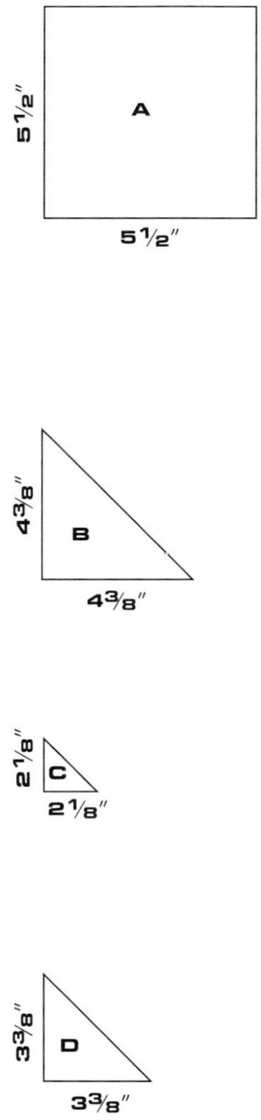

FIRST CUT			SECOND CUT		
			Number of Pieces		
Fabric and Yardage	Number of Pieces	Size	For 28 (45) Positive Blocks	For 28 (45) Negative Blocks	Shape
PLAIN PATCHES					
Yellow Solid 4 (5) yds.	5 (8)	5½″ × 40″	28 (45)	–	A
	7 (10)	4⅜″ × 40″	–	112 (180)	B
	7 (10)	2⅛″ × 40″	224 (360)	–	C
	5 (9)	3⅜″ × 40″	112 (180)	–	D
Dk. Green Solid 4 (5) yds.	5 (8)	5½″ × 40″	–	28 (45)	A
	7 (10)	4⅜″ × 40″	112 (180)	–	B
	7 (10)	2⅛″ × 40″	–	224 (360)	C
	5 (9)	3⅜″ × 40″	–	112 (180)	D
SPEEDY TRIANGLE SQUARES[1]					
Yellow Solid and Dk. Green Solid 2½ (3½) yds. each	9 (14)	18″ sq.	560 (900)	560 (900)	C/C

[1] See *Speedy Triangle Squares* on page 121. Mark 8 × 8 grids of 2⅛″ squares.

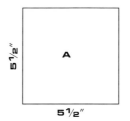

5½″ / 5½″ — A

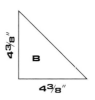

4⅜″ / 4⅜″ — B

2⅛″ / 2⅛″ — C

3⅜″ / 3⅜″ — D

GREAT SIZING TIPS

Because this pattern will repeat continuously no matter how many blocks are placed in each row or column, you can plan your quilt to be almost any size you wish. Just remember that the length of each edge will be a multiple of 10″ (one block). Some examples:

9 blocks in a 3 x 3 layout = 30″-square wallhanging

16 blocks in a 4 x 4 layout = 40″-square wallhanging

24 blocks in a 4 x 6 layout = 40″ x 60″ crib quilt

The size of this coverlet can be adjusted easily from twin to full/queen if the number of blocks is increased to make two additional rows and columns. Refer to the cutting chart, page 163, for the number of pieces to cut for the different sizes.

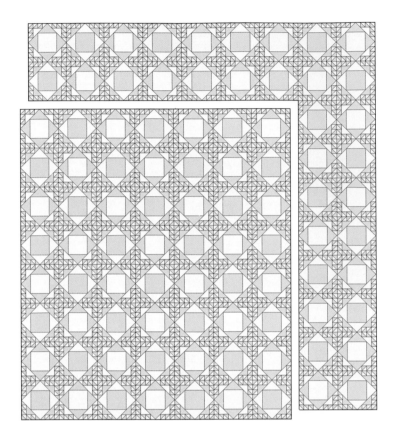

TWIN
56 blocks in a 7 × 8 layout

FULL/QUEEN
90 blocks in a 9 × 10 layout

BLOCK ASSEMBLY

Positive Block

Directions are given below for making one positive block. Amounts for making all 28 (twin) or 45 (full/queen) positive blocks at the same time are given in parentheses. Reverse fabric colors to make the same number of negative blocks.

COLOR KEY
☐ Yellow Solid
▧ Dk. green solid

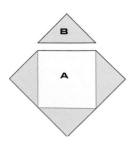

1. Sew 4 green B's to a yellow A to make one (28) (45) center square.

2. Join a C and 2 C/C squares to make one (112) (180) short strip.

3. Join a C and 3 C/C squares to make one (112) (180) long strip.

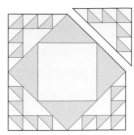

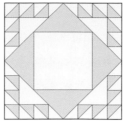

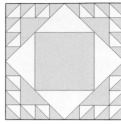

4. Sew short and long strips to a D to make 4 (112) (180) corner triangles.

5. Join units as shown.

FINISHED POSITIVE BLOCK

FINISHED NEGATIVE BLOCK

QUILT ASSEMBLY

Quilt Top

Arrange blocks as shown, alternating positive and negative blocks. Join blocks to make rows. Join rows.

TWIN

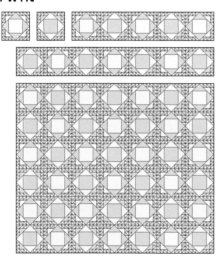

FULL/QUEEN

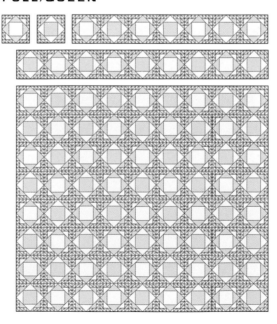

Finishing

1. Mark quilting design on each A square on quilt top, spacing pairs of lines 1⅜" apart.

2. Prepare batting and backing.

3. Assemble quilt layers.

4. Quilt on marked design lines and in-the-ditch on all seams.

5. Trim batting and backing to ½" beyond outermost seam line.

6. Bind quilt edges.

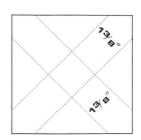

This pattern will look very different if you work with more than two colors. You might decide to make all the blocks the same, or make them all different. If you plan very carefully, you can use color to create the effect of a larger square or diamond within the overall scheme. If you do so, the four corners of a single block may be different colors.

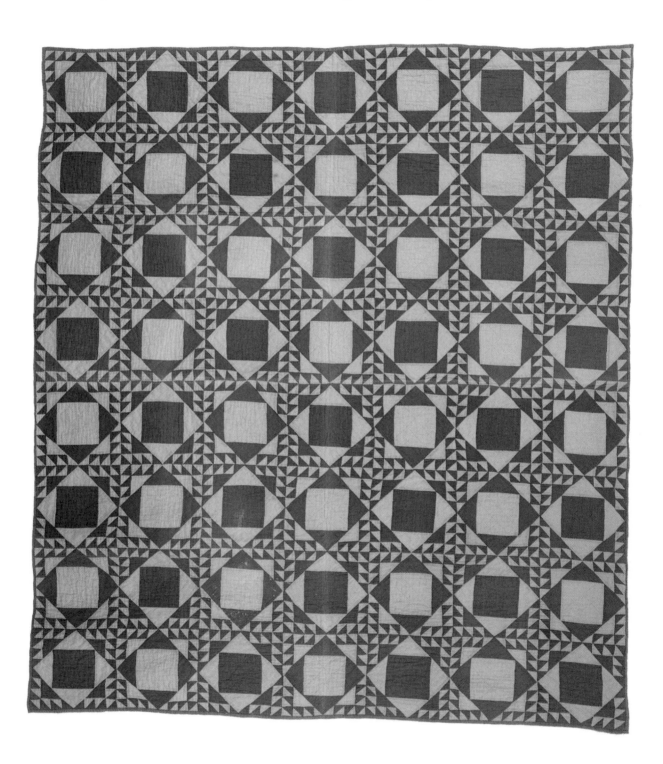

Photocopy this page, then create your own color scheme using colored pencils or markers. Refer to the examples on the previous page, or design a unique color arrangement to match your decor or please your fancy.

While the arrangement of the Pine Burr block featured here gives an allover pattern that is full of movement, it can be just as appealing when set in other ways. If you add sashing or plain patches between the blocks, the size of the quilt may change; you could compensate by using more or fewer blocks or adding borders.

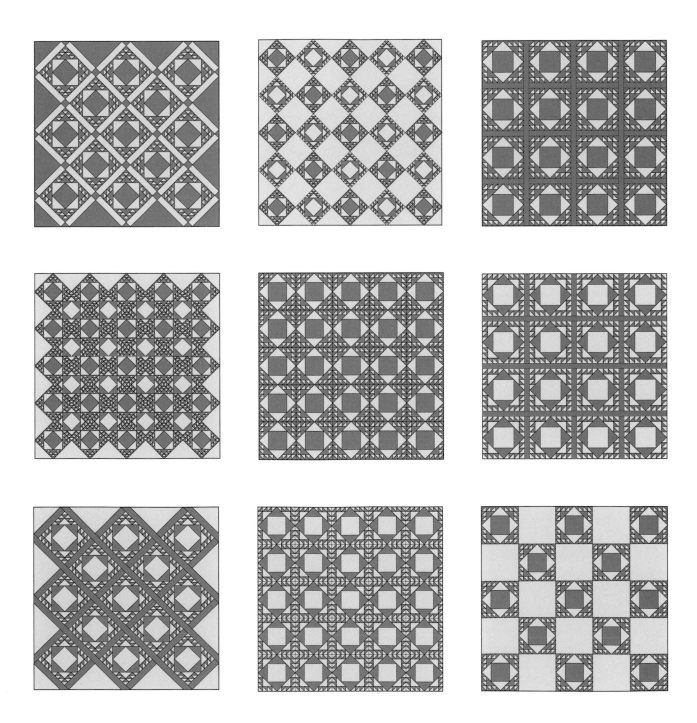

When You Wish

W̤hat doll could fail to dream sweetly under this exquisite little blanket of stars? Each of the simple eight-pointed stars is made from a different 1930s print. The fortunate creator of this tiny treasure inherited many of the fabrics from her grandmother, supplemented them with others purchased at a farm auction, and set them in perfect harmony with soft green and yellow solids.

Note: All dimensions are finished size. We have selected a representative color to depict the assorted prints on the blocks and pieced border. Refer to the photographs, opposite and page 176, to see the actual colors and their distribution.

BLOCK
12 blocks, 3⅜" square

SHORT SASHING STRIP
10 single arrows, 1" × 3⅞"

LONG SASHING STRIP
7 double arrows, 1" × 4⅜"

FIRST BORDER
Four ¼"-wide plain strips, cut to size and mitered

SECOND BORDER
Four 1"-wide pieced strips; side pieces added before top and bottom pieces

BINDING
Self-binding

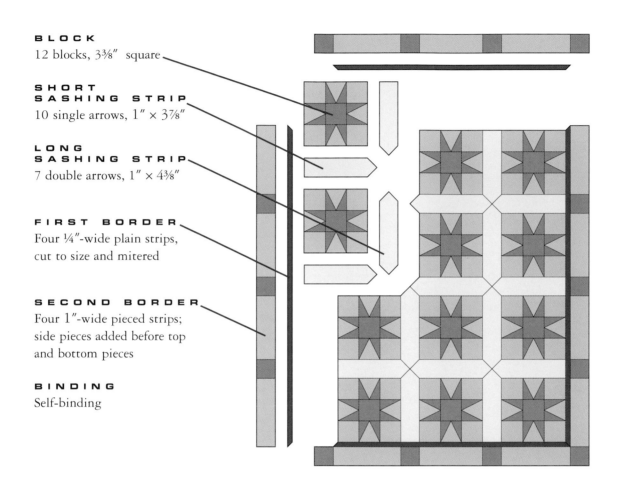

GREAT CUTTING TIPS

To cut the B and BR patches that form the points of the star, refer to the cutting chart for sizes and make three cuts, as follows:

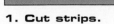

1. Cut strips.

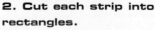

2. Cut each strip into rectangles.

3. Cut each rectangle into identical triangles.

Yardages are based on 44″-wide fabric. Amounts are given for making 12 identical blocks; amounts for making a single block are given in parentheses. Prepare templates, if desired, referring to drafting schematics. Cut strips and patches following cutting schematics and chart. Except for drafting schematics, which give finished sizes, all dimensions include ¼″ seam allowance and strips include extra length, unless otherwise stated.
(Note: Unmarked angles on cutting schematics are either 45° or 90°.)

DIMENSIONS

FINISHED BLOCK
3⅜″ square; about 4¾″ diagonal

FINISHED QUILT
14⅝″ × 19″

MATERIALS

LT. YELLOW SOLID
¼ yd.

OLIVE SOLID
¼ yd. (4″ × 6″)

PLUM SOLID
¼ yd.

ASSORTED PRINTS
Small amounts of at least 12 different prints to total about ¼ yd. (4″ × 6″)

SELF-BINDING
No extra fabric or cutting required.

BACKING *
¾ yd.

BATTING *

THREAD

*Backing and batting should be cut and pieced as necessary so they are at least 4″ larger than quilt on all sides, then trimmed to size after quilting.

DRAFTING SCHEMATICS

(No seam allowance added)

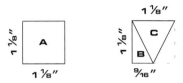

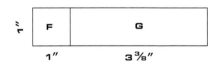
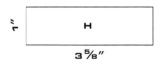

FIRST CUT			SECOND CUT	
Fabric and Yardage	Number of Pieces	Size	Number of Pieces	Shape
PATCHES				
Assorted Prints* ¼ yd.	3 (1)	1⅝″ × 10″	12 (1)	A
	6 (1)	1¼″ × 10″	48 (4)	B
			48 (4)	B_R
	2	1½″ × 20″	14	F
Olive solid ¼ yd.	10 (1)	1⅝″ × 10″	48 (4)	A
	6 (1)	1⅞″ × 10″	48 (4)	C
	2	1½″ × 20″	6	G
	2	1½″ × 20″	8	H
Lt. Yellow Solid ¼ yd.	3	1½″ × 20″	10	D
	3	1½″ × 20″	7	E
FIRST BORDER				
Plum Solid ¼ yd.	2	¾″ × 16″		
	2	¾″ × 20″		

*Cut B and B_R patches from same strips; see the *Great Cutting Tips*, page 171.

CUTTING SCHEMATICS

(Seam allowance included)

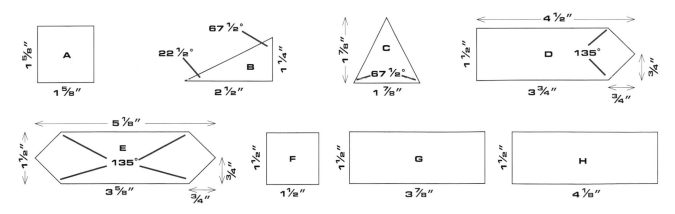

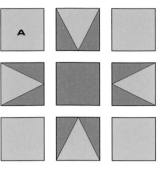

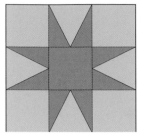

FINISHED BLOCK

1. Join a B and a B_R to a C, to make a pieced square. Make 48.

2. Arrange units as shown to make 3 rows. Join rows. Make 12.

Quilt Center

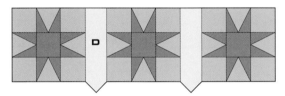

1. Join 3 blocks and 2 D's to make a narrow strip. Make 2.

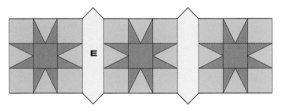

2. Join 3 blocks and 2 E's to make a wide strip. Make 2.

3. Arrange units as shown at right. Join units by setting them in, one row at a time.

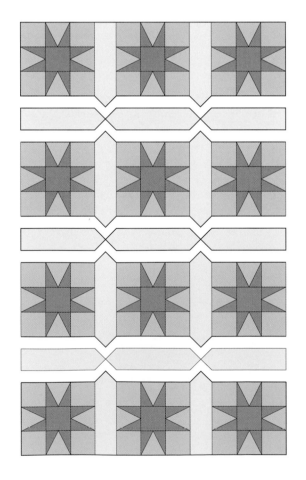

Borders

1. Join first border to quilt, mitering corners.
2. Make second border.

◆ Join 4 F's, 2 H's, and a G as shown to make a short strip. Make 2.

◆ Join 2 H's, 3 F's, and 2 G's as shown to make a long strip. Make 2.

3. Join second border to quilt, first long strips at sides, then short strips at top and bottom, as shown at right.

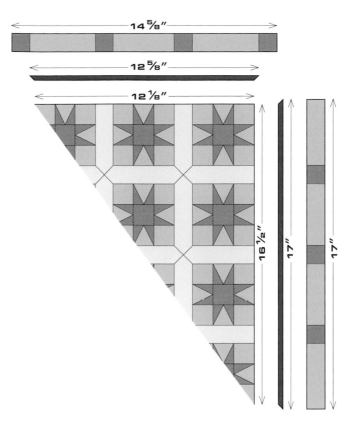

Finishing

1. Prepare batting and backing.
2. Assemble quilt layers.
3. Bind quilt edges.
◆ Trim batting even with outer-most seam line. Trim quilt top and backing to ¼" beyond batting.
◆ Press under ¼" at edges of quilt top and backing, align folds, and slipstitch together.
4. Single-outline quilt as shown.
◆ *For quilt center:* Quilt ¼" from all edges of lt. yellow and olive patches.
◆ *For second border:* Quilt ¼" from outer seam line.

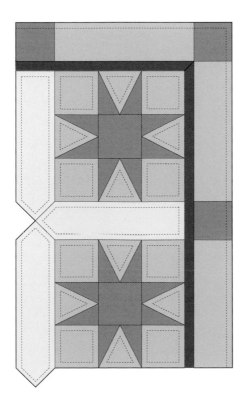

Use stronger colors to emphasize the graphic quality of this design, softer ones to keep it sweet. You could use three or four colors in each block, or stay with two and make the sashing match the stars. Or make the sashing and borders from one color family, and then alternate positive/negative blocks from another.

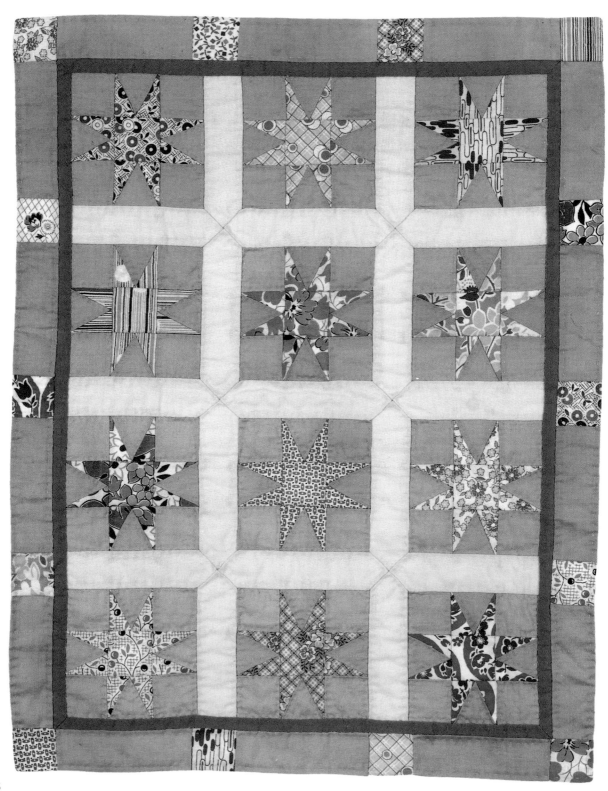

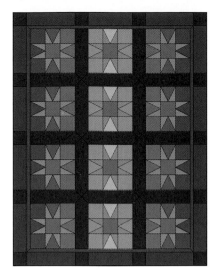

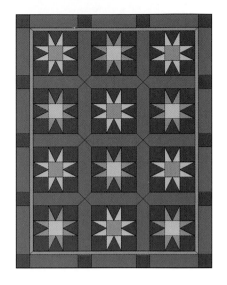

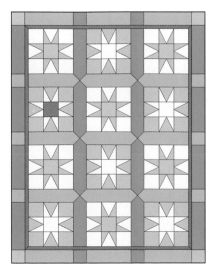

Winter Storm Warning

This wallhanging was begun in a workshop in which the participants turned and rearranged triangles to achieve different effects. Polly Whitehorn found that her piece had the quality of a wintry landscape. She added freehand machine-stitching to delineate a tree and fence, and used tiny iridescent beads to represent snowflakes. The hanging is quilted in a swirling pattern that evokes the winds.

Note: All dimensions except for binding are finished size.

PLAIN BLOCK
14 blocks, 3″ square

BORDER
4 strips, 2″ wide, cut to size

BINDING
1½″-wide strip, pieced as necessary and cut to size

PIECED BLOCK
16 blocks, 3″ square

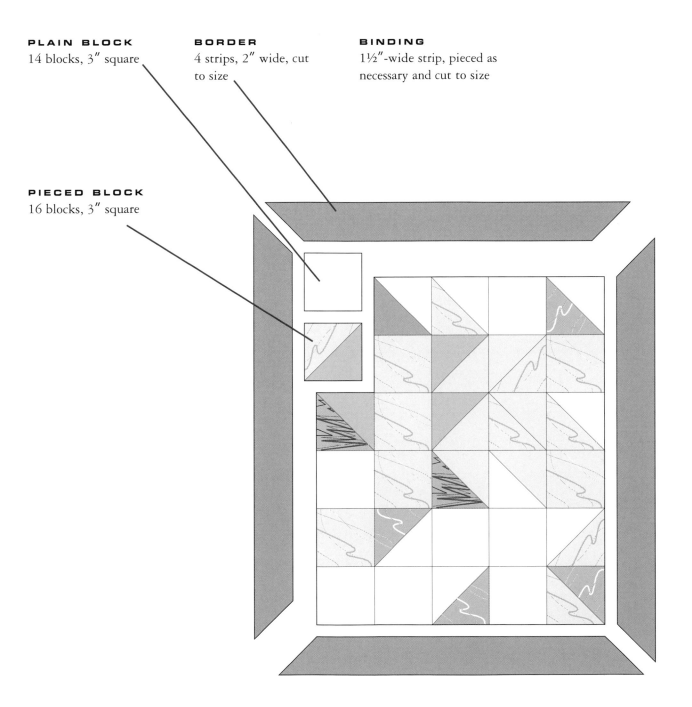

Note: Diagram on page 179 shows quilt one-third of actual size.

Yardages are based on 44″-wide fabric. Prepare templates, if desired, referring to drafting schematics. Cut strips and patches following schematics and chart. Cut binding as directed below. Except for drafting schematics, which give finished sizes, all dimensions include ¼″ seam allowance and strips include extra length, unless otherwise stated. (Note: Angles on all patches in this project are either 45° or 90°.)

DIMENSIONS

FINISHED BLOCK
3″ square, about 4¼″ diagonal

FINISHED WALLHANGING
19″ × 22″

MATERIALS

- **WHITE SOLID**
  ¼ yd.
- **LT. GRAY PRINT**
  ¼ yd.
- **LT./DK. PURPLE PRINT**
  ¼ yd.
- **DK. MAUVE SOLID**
  ¼ yd.
- **BROWN/LAVENDER PRINT**
  ¼ yd.
- **LT. BLUE/LAVENDER PRINT**
  ¼ yd.
- **MAROON PRINT**
  ¼ yd.
- **DK. GRAY SOLID**
  ¾ yd.
- **BACKING** *
  ¾ yd.
- **BATTING** *
- **THREAD**
- **TINY BEADS**
  100 white iridescent
- **BINDING**
  Use ¼ yd. black
  solid to make a
  1½″ × 92″ strip.

*Backing and batting should be cut and pieced as necessary so they are at least 4″ larger than quilt top on all sides, then trimmed to size after quilting.

DRAFTING SCHEMATICS

(No seam allowance added)

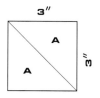

CUTTING SCHEMATICS

(Seam allowance included)

3⁷⁄₈″

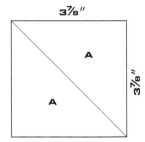

3⁷⁄₈″

3½″

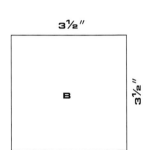

3½″

	FIRST CUT		SECOND CUT	
Fabric and Yardage	Number of Pieces	Size	Number of Pieces	Shape
PLAIN PATCHES				
White ¼ yd.	1	3⁷⁄₈″ × 20″	8	A
	1	3½″ × 40″	8	B
Lt. Gray ¼ yd.	1	3⁷⁄₈″ × 20″	6	A
Lt./Dk. Purple ¼ yd.	—	—	1	A
Dk. Mauve ¼ yd.	1	3⁷⁄₈″ × 10″	4	A
Brown/ Lavender ¼ yd.	1	3⁷⁄₈″ × 10″	4	A
Lt. Blue/ Lavender ¼ yd.	1	3⁷⁄₈″ × 20″	7	A
	1	3½″ × 40″	6	B
Maroon ¼ yd.	1	3⁷⁄₈″ × 10″	2	A
BORDERS				
Dk. Gray ½ yd.	2	2½″ × 29″		
	2	2½″ × 32″		

GREAT SIZING TIPS

Because this hanging is made from such simple blocks (a plain square and a same-size triangle square) it is very easy to change the size of your hanging by changing the block size. Decide how long you want your hanging to be (less any borders) and divide that dimension by the number of rows in the assembly diagram. The result will be the finished size of the square (the length of the perpendicular legs of the triangle) with which you should work. (Multiply this by the number of columns across the assembly diagram to find the width of your hanging.)

For example, to make a hanging 30″ long:
30″ divided by 6 rows = 5″ squares or triangles; when multiplied by 5 columns, you see that the hanging will be 25″ wide. Be sure to add the width of the borders to your final calculations and also to add seam allowance before cutting your pieces.

COLOR KEY

- ☐ White solid
- ☐ Lt. gray print
- ☐ Lt./dk. purple print
- ☐ Dk. mauve solid
- ◨ Brown/lavender print
- ◨ Lt. blue/lavender print
- ▨ Maroon print
- ☐ Dk. gray solid

Pieced Block

Join A's in pairs to make A/A squares as shown in the chart.

NUMBER TO MAKE	COLOR COMBINATION
1	White and lt. gray
1	White and lt./dk. purple
3	White and brown/lavender
3	White and lt. blue/lavender
2	Lt. gray and dk. mauve
1	Lt. gray and maroon
2	Lt. gray and lt. blue/lavender
1	Lt. blue/lavender and dk. mauve
1	Lt. blue/lavender and brown/lavender
1	Dk. mauve and maroon

FINISHED PIECED BLOCK

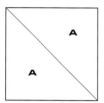

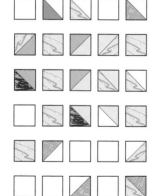

Quilt Center

Arrange pieced and plain blocks as shown. Join blocks to make 6 rows. Join rows.

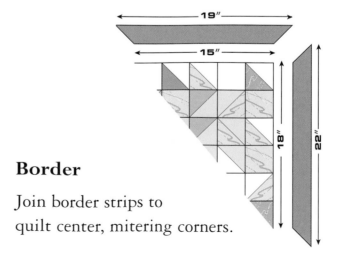

Border

Join border strips to quilt center, mitering corners.

Finishing

1. Mark designs on quilt top: Mark tree, fence, and grass on quilt center. Mark swirls of wind on quilt center and border.

2. Make black tree, fence, and grass with free-machine embroidery, straight-stitch hand-embroidery, or indelible fine-point pen.

3. Prepare batting and backing.

4. Assemble layers for quilting.

5. Quilt swirls of wind with white, iridescent blue, and gold metallic threads.

6. Trim batting and backing to ½″ beyond outermost seam line.

7. Bind quilt edges.

8. Sew a sprinkling of bead "snowflakes" all over quilt center, making sure stitches don't go through to back of quilt.

Give yourself time to experiment with the effects of color and layout on design. Follow the directions for our hanging using the palette of your choice: Lay out the pieces, and before you sew any of them together, rearrange them until you are pleased with the effect.

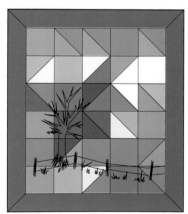

Lady of the Lake Quilt

This is a classic pattern with the blocks set on point and rotated so that both the large and small red and white triangles seem to spin, giving the quilt a sense of movement. Pinwheels and hourglasses appear where the corners of the blocks meet. The Rocky Glen quilt folded on the trunk is a variation of this pattern; *see page 196 for directions.*

Note: All dimensions except for binding are finished size.
Amounts for full/queen are given in parentheses.

DARK HALF-BLOCK
8 (10) half-blocks, 13½″ on two sides, about 19⅛″ on third side

BINDING
1½″-wide strip pieced as necessary and cut to size

WHOLE BLOCK
24 (40) blocks, 13½″ square

LIGHT HALF-BLOCK
8 (10) half-blocks, 13½″ on two sides, about 19⅛″ on third side

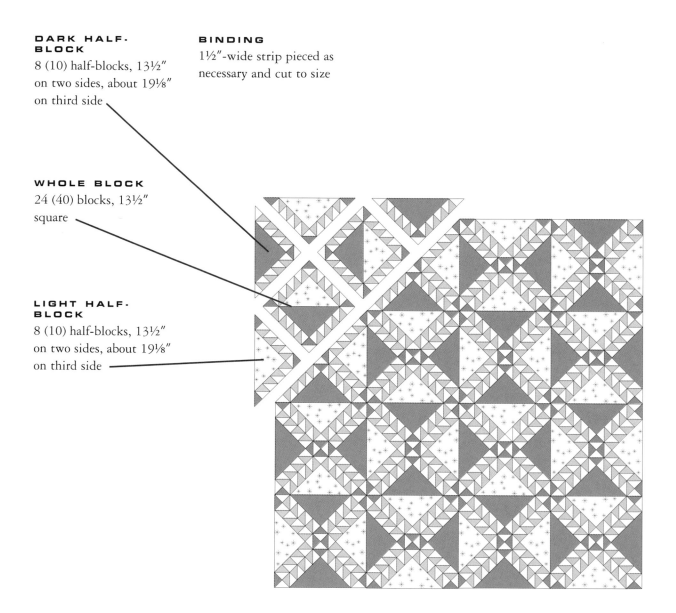

Note: Sizes and amounts for full/queen are given in parentheses.

Yardages are based on 44″-wide fabric. Prepare templates, if desired, referring to drafting schematic. Cut strips and patches following schematics and chart. Except for drafting schematic, which gives finished sizes, all dimensions include ¼″ seam allowance and strips include extra length, unless otherwise stated. (Note: Angles on all patches in this project are either 45° or 90°.)

DIMENSIONS

FINISHED BLOCK

13½″ square, about 19⅛″ diagonal

FINISHED QUILT

76½″ (95⅝″) square

MATERIALS

- **MUSLIN SOLID**
  3¼ (4) yds.

- **RED SOLID**
  2½ (4) yds.

- **FOUR (FIVE) TINY RED-ON-EGGSHELL PRINTS**
  1 yd. each

- **EIGHT BROWN AND/OR RED ALLOVER PRINTS**
  ¼ yd. each

- **BACKING ***
  5 (9) yds.

- **BATTING ***

- **THREAD**

- **BINDING**
  Use ½ yd. red solid to make a 1½″ × 320″ (1½″ × 430″) strip.

*Backing and batting should be cut and pieced as necessary so they are at least 4″ larger than quilt top on all sides, then trimmed to size after quilting.

DRAFTING SCHEMATIC

(No seam allowance added)

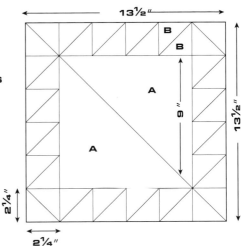

CUTTING SCHEMATICS

(Seam allowance included)

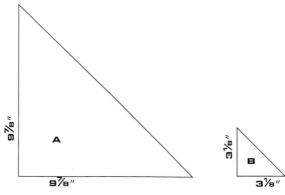

	FIRST CUT		SECOND CUT			
			Number of Pieces			
Fabric and Yardage	Number of Pieces	Size	For 24 (40) Whole Blocks	For 8 (10) Light Half-Blocks	For 8 (10) Dark Half-Blocks	Shape
PLAIN PATCHES						
Red Solid ½ (¾) yd.	1 (2)	9⅞" × 40"	—	8 (10)	—	A
	1 (2)	3⅛" × 40"	—	16 (20)	—	B
Red-on-Eggshell Prints ½ yd. each	4 (5)	9⅞" sq.	—	—	8 (10)	A[1]
Muslin Solid ¼ yd.	1	3⅛" × 40"	—	—	16 (20)	B
SPEEDY TRIANGLE SQUARES[2]						
Red Solid 1 (1¾) yd. and Red-on-Eggshell Prints ½ yd. each	6 (10)	10⅞" × 20¾"	24 (40)	—	—	A/A[3]
Red Solid and Muslin Solid ½ (1) yd. each	2 (3)	16⅝" × 19¾"	96 (160)	8 (10)	8 (10)	B/B[4]
Muslin Solid 1½ (1¾) yds. and Brown/Red Prints ¼ yd. each	8 (14)	13½" × 19¾"	384 (640)	—	—	B/B[5]
	8 (10)	4⅛" × 13½"	—	64 (80)	64 (80)	B/B[6]

[1] Cut strips from 4 (5) different prints.

[2] See *Speedy Triangle Squares* on page 221.

[3] Mark 1 × 2 grids with 9⅞" squares on 4 (5) different prints.

[4] Mark 5 × 6 grids with 3⅛" squares.

[5] Mark 4 × 6 grids with 3⅛" squares on 8 different prints.

[6] Mark 4 × 6 grids with 3⅛" squares on 8 different prints.

The size of this coverlet can be adjusted easily from twin to full/queen if the number of whole and partial blocks is increased to make two additional center rows. Refer to the cutting chart, previous page, for the number of pieces to cut for the different sizes.

TWIN
24 whole blocks, 8 light and 8 dark half-blocks

FULL/QUEEN
40 whole blocks, 10 light and 10 dark half-blocks

You could use four Lady of the Lake blocks, (or four half-blocks), to make a wallhanging. Refer to *Changing Colors* and *Changing Sets*, pages 192-195, for some ideas, and use the line drawing to work out a configuration that appeals to you.

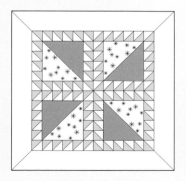
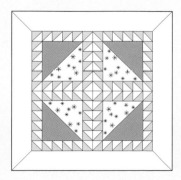

Whole Block

Directions are given below for making one whole block. Amounts for making all 24 (twin) or 40 (full/queen) whole blocks at the same time are given in parentheses.

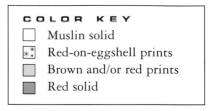

COLOR KEY
☐ Muslin solid
▦ Red-on-eggshell prints
▨ Brown and/or red prints
■ Red solid

  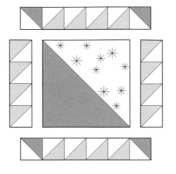 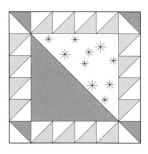

1. Join 4 print-and-solid B/B's and 2 solid B/B's to make 2 (48) (80) long strips.

2. Join 4 print-and-solid B/B's to make 2 (48) (80) short strips.

3. Arrange pieced units as shown. Join to make 3 rows. Join rows.

FINISHED WHOLE BLOCK

Half-block

(Make 8 each of light and dark half-blocks for twin, 10 each for full/queen.) Stitch patches into units following sequence of whole block. Arrange pieced units as shown. Join to make 3 rows. Join rows.

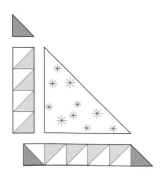  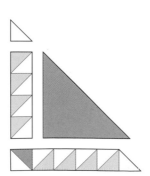 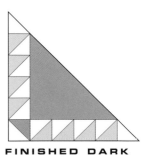

FINISHED LIGHT HALF-BLOCK

FINISHED DARK HALF-BLOCK

Quilt Top

Arrange whole and partial blocks as shown. Join units to make rows. Join rows.

TWIN

FULL/QUEEN

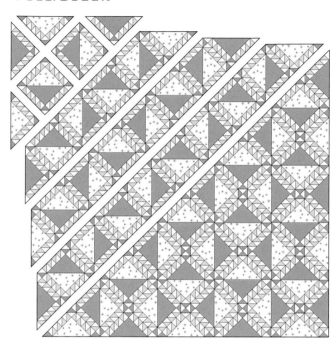

Finishing

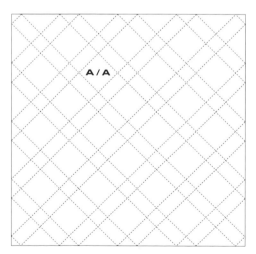

1. Prepare batting and backing.

2. Assemble quilt layers.

3. Quilt in-the-ditch on seams around all A/A's, extending quilting lines completely across quilt.

4. Trim backing and batting to ½" beyond outermost seam line.

5. Bind quilt edges.

Whether you use assorted or matching fabrics for your sawtooth strips, make all the corners from two contrasting colors to get the full effect of pinwheels and hourglasses dancing across the surface.

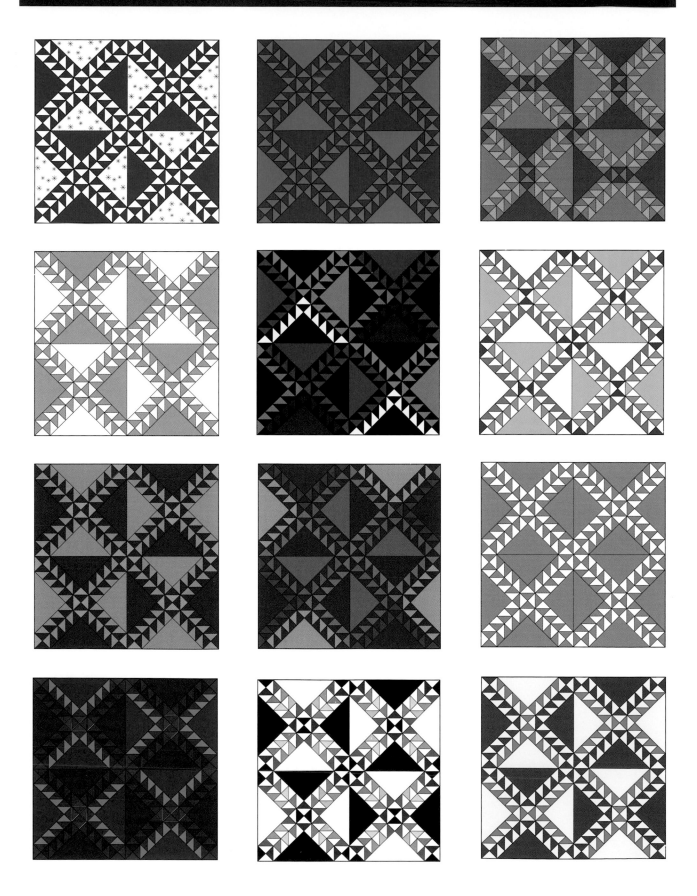

P hotocopy this page, then create your own color scheme using colored pencils or markers. Refer to the examples on the previous pages, or design a unique arrangement to match your decor or please your fancy.

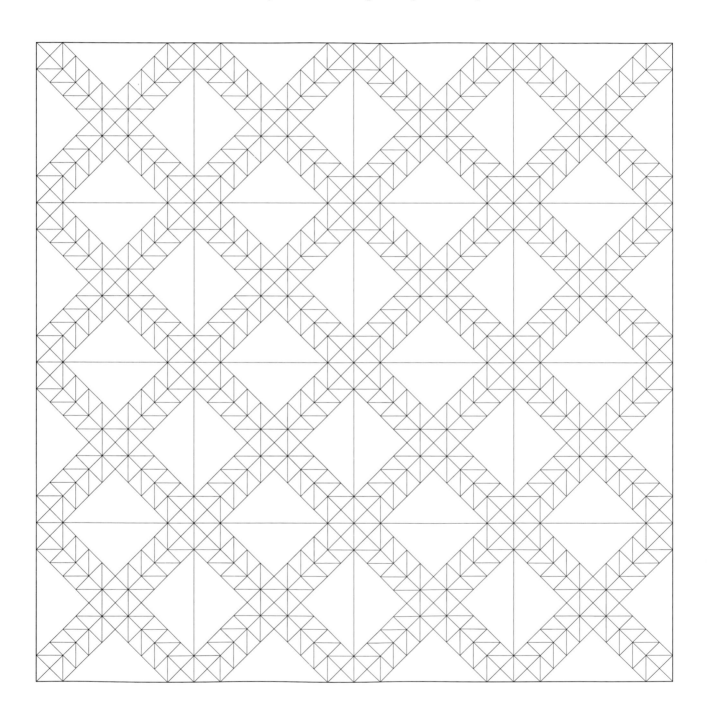

If you vary the setting angle from diagonal to straight, add sashing, or change the alternation of light and dark fabrics, you can create many intriguing allover patterns from the Lady of the Lake block. Note how different the pattern looks with plain or pieced alternate blocks. These variations may change the size of the quilt; you could compensate by using more or fewer blocks or adding borders.

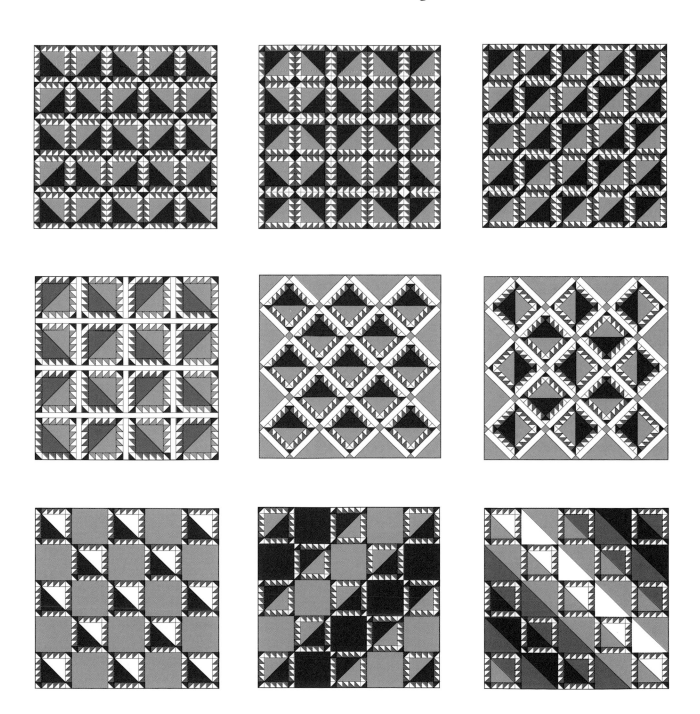

Rocky Glen Quilt

If you change the orientation of the small triangle squares for each block as shown, you will have a Rocky Glen block. In the quilt pictured here, the number and size of the blocks are different from ours, but you can use our instructions and this lovely antique as an inspiration for making your own unique variation.

Change the set from diagonal to straight and add a single border of small pieced squares to create symmetrical framing of the larger pieced squares. You can also arrange the blocks (and half-blocks) in the same manner as for our quilt. See also *Changing Colors*, page 192, for more great suggestions.

Use the chart below to plan a straight-set Rocky Glen (or Lady of the Lake) quilt.

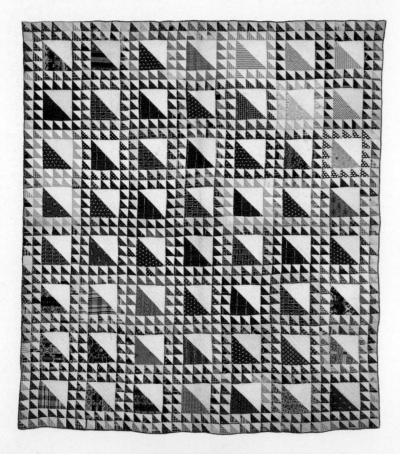

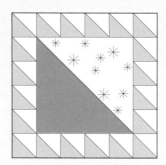

WHOLE BLOCK

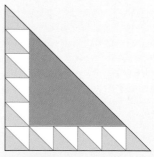

DARK HALF-BLOCK

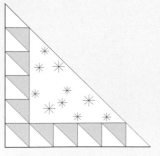

LIGHT HALF-BLOCK

STRAIGHT SETS			
Number of Blocks	Block Layout	Size without Border	Size with One Border
25	5″ × 5″	67½″ square	72″ square
36	6″ × 6″	81″ square	85½″ square
49	7″ × 7″	94½″ square	99″ square
64	8″ × 8″	108″ square	112½″ square

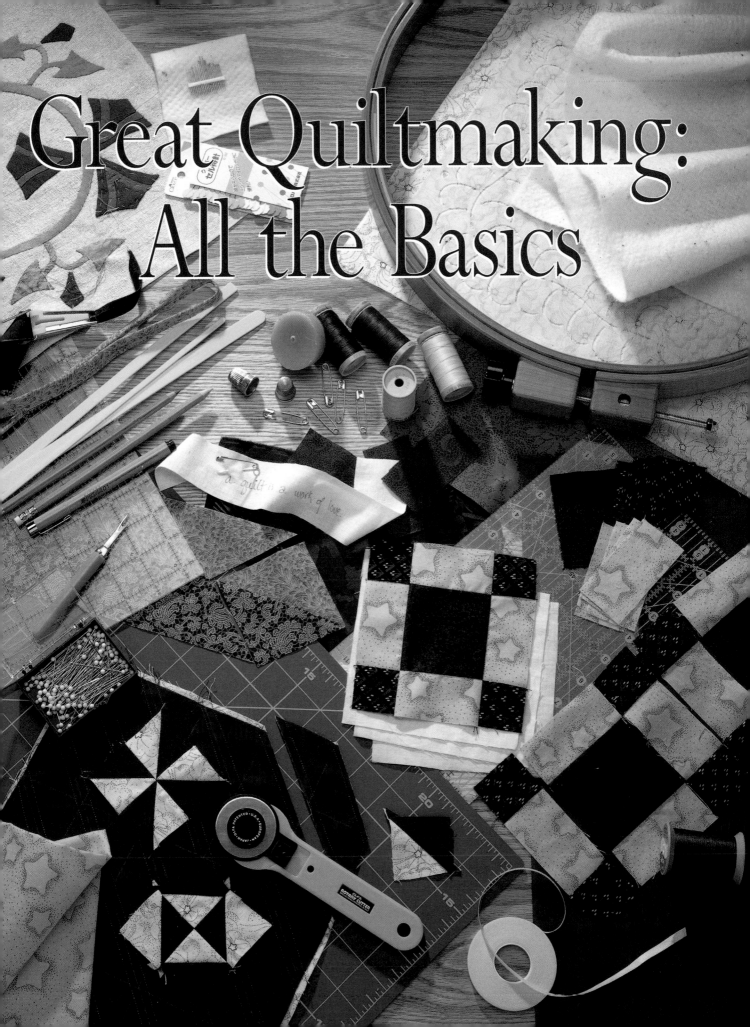

Great Quiltmaking: All the Basics

Tools and Equipment

*P*recision is a must in quiltmaking. Using the appropriate tools and equipment for measuring, marking, cutting, and stitching will make each step in the process more accurate, faster, and more enjoyable. Tools for measuring and drafting can be found in most fabric, crafts, and art supply stores. (Note: Be sure always to follow the manufacturer's directions.)

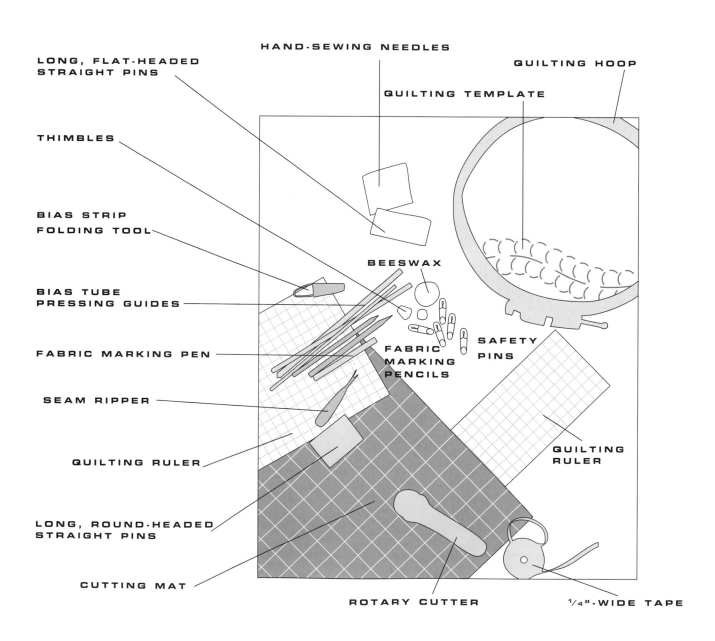

HAND-SEWING NEEDLES

QUILTING HOOP

LONG, FLAT-HEADED STRAIGHT PINS

QUILTING TEMPLATE

THIMBLES

BIAS STRIP FOLDING TOOL

BEESWAX

BIAS TUBE PRESSING GUIDES

SAFETY PINS

FABRIC MARKING PENCILS

FABRIC MARKING PEN

QUILTING RULER

SEAM RIPPER

QUILTING RULER

LONG, ROUND-HEADED STRAIGHT PINS

CUTTING MAT

ROTARY CUTTER

¼"-WIDE TAPE

FOR MEASURING AND DRAFTING

◆ **RULER:**
Used for measuring at every stage of quiltmaking. You will need at least two: 18″ or 24″, and a yardstick. If your rulers will be used as an aid in marking straight lines, make sure edges are smooth and nick-free. Metal rulers are more durable than those made of wood or plastic.

◆ **T-SQUARE:**
Used to measure and make 90° angles. Also, L-shaped rulers serve the same purpose.

◆ **COMPASS:**
Used to mark whole and partial circles. Most drafting compasses can be used for circles up to 12″ in diameter. For larger circles, a beam compass or a string-and-pencil compass can be used.

◆ **PROTRACTOR:**
Used to measure angles that can't be verified with other measuring tools or graph paper.

FOR MAKING PATTERNS AND TEMPLATES

Accuracy in making a quilt begins with the patterns and templates used to mark the pieces and designs on fabric. Commercially prepared templates made of cardboard, plastic, or metal are available for the most common shapes and sizes of pieces, but if you make your own patterns and templates (see pages 217-218, "Preparing Patterns and Templates"), you will need at least some of the following:

◆ **TRACING PAPER:**
Used for copying by hand the patterns that are provided in individual project directions. Tracing-paper copying is an inexpensive (but potentially time-consuming) alternative to photocopying.

◆ **GRAPH PAPER:**
Used for drafting or enlarging patterns. The most useful grid sizes are those that correspond to markings on your ruler (⅛″, ¼″, ½″, and 1″).

◆ **POSTERBOARD:**
Used for making templates. Patterns are glued or drafted directly on posterboard and then cut out with a crafts knife.

◆ **SANDPAPER:**
Used as a nonslip backing for posterboard templates and also as a template by itself. Sandpaper templates cannot be used for reverse pieces (rough side up) without sacrificing their gripping quality.

◆ **MYLAR:**
Used for making templates. Mylar is a clear, relatively thin but durable plastic that many quilters use. It can be cut with scissors or a crafts knife.

◆ **TEMPLATE PLASTIC:**
Used for making templates. Template plastic comes in clear and semi-transparent types, in light and medium

weights that can be cut with a sturdy pair of scissors. Lightweight plastic can also be cut with a crafts knife, which makes it a good choice for curved-edge templates. Medium-weight plastic sometimes comes with a square grid on it, making it useful for drafting patterns directly on the plastic and for verifying 90° angles.

◆ **FREEZER PAPER:**
Used to back fabric shapes for appliqué and English paper-piecing.

FOR MARKING FABRIC

There is an almost limitless variety of tools and methods for marking fabric. Remember, though, that markings should be visible as guides only when you need them and unseen when you are finished with them. Use a fine-pointed nonpermanent marker (black, white, or a color) that contrasts with the fabric, and test it to make sure marked lines will vanish from the fabric.

◆ **CHALK:**
Used for marking around templates or along a ruler or other straight edge. Chalk comes in different colors, but it can be messy to use (and sometimes hard to remove from fabric). There are chalk dispensers designed especially for sewing that enable you to mark thin, visible lines and still keep your hands, fabric, and work surface clean. Stamping powder can be used for the same purpose.

◆ **PENCILS:**
Used primarily for marking around templates, along a ruler or other straight edge, or with a compass. Lead pencils and chalk pencils are generally preferred for this type of marking.

◆ **PENS:**
Used for marking around templates or along a ruler or other straight edge. There are two types of non-permanent inks for fabric: those that fade over time and those that wash out. Pens with fading ink make lines that may disappear before you're finished with them. Those that wash out may require repeated washings before they vanish totally.

◆ **DRESSMAKER'S CARBON (TRACING) PAPER:**
Used for transferring design lines and pattern markings. Dressmaker's carbon is thicker and sturdier than ordinary clerical carbon paper and is available in various colors in fabric and crafts stores. To transfer designs, use a blunt pencil or stylus, a dry ball-point pen, or tracing wheel (similar to a pizza cutter, but with a blunt serrated edge).

◆ **TAPE:**
Used to mark straight and/or equidistant lines, usually for quilting. Drafting, masking, or quilting tape that is ¼″ wide can be used for marking seam lines or lines for single-outline, double-outline, echo, or diagonal quilting.

◆ **BACKLIGHTING:**
Used behind a pattern or design and the paper or fabric to which it will be transferred, to create a translucency that makes the design lines visible on the front for

marking. You can tape the design and fabric to a clean window on a sunny day, place them over a pane of glass backlit by an ordinary light bulb (not so close as to burn the design, fabric, and/or your fingers), or use a light box (available in art and photo supply stores).

◆ **WEIGHTS:**
Used to prevent templates from shifting around on fabric during marking (or cutting). Flat, lead shapes can be found in fabric and crafts stores, and you can also use whatever you have on hand that is an appropriate size and shape to do the job.

FOR GENERAL CUTTING

Whatever you want to cut, it is essential to have the right tools. Use each type of cutter only for the purpose for which it is intended, and keep your cutters as sharp as possible to make predictably smooth, even cuts.

Scissors and Knives

◆ **ALL-PURPOSE SCISSORS:**
Used for cutting anything but fabric. Designate a pair of good-quality, sturdy, all-purpose scissors for cutting paper, cardboard, plastic, and other sewing and crafts needs.

◆ **SEWING SCISSORS (SHEARS):**
Used for cutting fabric only. Reserve a pair of scissors just for fabric, to prevent dulling or nicking the blades on other materials. Available for either left- or right-handed people (and also for people who have difficulty in gripping), sewing scissors are designed so that one blade can lie flat against the work surface while the other blade goes up and down.

◆ **EMBROIDERY SCISSORS:**
Used for cutting thread of all types. Embroidery scissors are small and straight-bladed. Keep them handy whenever sewing.

◆ **APPLIQUÉ SCISSORS:**
Used for cutting appliqués and other curved fabric pieces. Appliqué scissors are small like embroidery scissors but have delicate, sharply pointed curved blades that make them ideal for cutting even the most intricate of shapes.

◆ **CRAFTS KNIFE:**
Used for cutting paper, cardboard, plastic, tape, etc. A crafts knife consists of an angled blade in a special holder that not only secures the blade but also acts as a handle to keep fingers away from the sharp edge of the knife.

Never use a single-edge razor blade as a substitute for a crafts knife. Instead, keep an adequate supply of blades on hand for your knife and change blades as often as needed, disposing of the used ones safely.

FOR ROTARY CUTTING

Rotary cutters, self-healing cutting mats, and special rulers all make cutting fabric pieces faster, easier, and more accurate than ever before. Experiment with your rulers to learn how to align their markings with the edges of your fabric in order to cut the different shapes and sizes you will need.

Cutters

A rotary cutter resembles a pizza cutter, but it also has a built-in guard to shield the sharp blade when not in use. On some rotary cutters the guard is withdrawn for use and extended for storage. On others it is the blade that extends and retracts.

Some cutters fit more comfortably in the hand than others, and the amount of pressure required to extend and retract the guard (or blade) can vary from brand to brand, so try out several different types before buying one.

Always stand up when doing rotary cutting, to have a better view of the fabric and more control over the ruler and cutter.

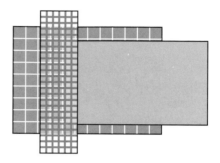

1. Place fabric on cutting mat and line up ruler on fabric.

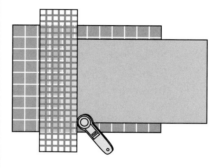

2. With one hand holding the ruler firmly in position, remove cutter guard (or extend blade) with your other hand, and place blade parallel to and snugly against edge of ruler, perpendicular to cutting mat.

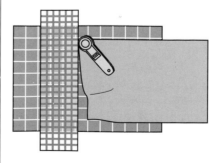

3. Press down on cutter and roll it away from you in one smooth motion, maintaining uniform pressure.
4. Replace guard (or retract blade) after use.

SAFETY TIPS

♦ A rotary cutter is a very sharp tool that should be treated with care at all times.
♦ Make sure the blade is protected whenever you put down the cutter.
♦ Keep fingers (and anything else you don't want to cut) away from an unprotected blade.
♦ Keep rotary cutters out of the reach of children.
♦ Cut away from yourself, never toward you.
♦ Never use a rotary cutter to cut anything but fabric.
♦ Carefully clean or replace blades as soon as they begin to show wear by skipping along fabric instead of cutting smoothly and cleanly.

Mats

Rotary cutting should be done on a flat, level surface at a height that is comfortable for you while standing up, such as a dining table, work table, or countertop. Always use a self-healing cutting mat to protect your work surface from the sharp blade.

Some cutting mats have a square grid on one side (usually 1″ squares) with edges marked off in ⅛″ increments and one or more 45° angle lines. At least one side of the mat should have a slightly rough surface, to help keep fabric from shifting during cutting.

Use a mat large enough to accommodate a 44″-wide piece of fabric folded in half, such as one that measures 18″ x 24″ or 24″ x 36″.

Store cutting mats flat, away from direct sunlight and excessive heat.

Rulers

There are many different rulers and templates available for rotary cutting, but rather than buy a separate one for each shape and size piece you want to cut, you can get the same results with just a few basic, general-purpose rulers.

The most useful rulers are made of heavy, clear plastic or acrylic and are 1/16″ to ⅛″ thick with straight, smooth edges that will stand up to miles of rotary cutting. Rulers should have markings on one surface in increments of ⅛″, ¼″, ½″, and 1″ (some have 1/16″ increments, too), and a grid (usually of 1″ squares) all over. They should also have one or more angled lines. (Note: You can add any markings that your rulers might be missing with a permanent marker.)

♦ **RECTANGULAR RULER:**
Used for cutting strips and other shapes, and for straightening fabric edges. Look for rulers that have at least several angled lines (30°, 45°, 60°, 120°, or 135°) in addition to a square grid. Large rulers (at least 6″ wide and 18″ to 24″ long) are the most versatile. Small rulers (2″ to 6″ wide and 6″ to 18″ long) are lighter in weight than large ones and are handy for cutting small pieces.

♦ **SQUARE RULER:**
Used for cutting squares and rectangles. Whether small (6″ to 8″ square) or large (10″ to 15″ square), each ruler should have a 45° diagonal line running from corner to corner so it can also be used for cutting triangles, bias squares, bias rectangles, and other shapes that rely on 45° angles.

♦ **DRAFTING TRIANGLE:**
Used for cutting 45° and 90° lines and for straightening fabric edges. Drafting rulers for rotary cutting can be made of either plastic or sturdy metal, but metal may damage cutter blades.

♦ **DIAMOND RULER:**
Used for cutting triangles, diamonds, and other non-rectilinear shapes. A 60° diamond ruler can be used for cutting 30°, 60°, and 120° angles.

Tape

Tape is useful for protecting rulers from wear, preventing them from slipping around on fabric, and for marking outlines of shapes directly on them. Use short strips of a masking, drafting, or quilter's tape that is ¼″ wide and easily removed from plastic. Whether you place the tape on the marked or unmarked side of a ruler depends on your reason for applying it.

♦ **ON THE MARKED SIDE:**
Used between markings so that the ruler will be elevated and the markings not touching the fabric when the ruler is placed marked side down on it. (Note: Unless care is taken, the markings on most rulers will eventually begin to peel or wear away. They can also be pulled off by tape, so never place tape directly on top of them.)

♦ **ON THE UNMARKED SIDE:**
Used to help prevent the ruler from slipping around (when positioned with the unmarked side down) on fabric. Tape can also be used to mark template shapes directly on the unmarked side of the ruler (for use with the marked side down on fabric).

FOR SECURING FABRIC

Different steps in the quiltmaking process require different methods of securing fabric. Use the appropriate equipment (pins, fabric adhesives, hoops/frames) for each step, and remember that pinning first is faster than picking out poor seams.

Pins

Pins must be sharp (for ease in piercing fabric), fine (for preventing noticeable holes in fabric), and rustproof (to prevent rust from making pins difficult to slide through and/or staining fabric). Silk pins and ballpoint pins are the sharpest.

♦ **STRAIGHT PINS:**
For patchwork and appliqué, some people prefer tiny straight pins (sequin pins), because they are very fine and short. Some find that standard-size pins work well for most sewing needs, and others prefer to use extra-long straight pins for holding the quilt layers together for basting.

Whatever length pins you use, you might want to get the kind that have large, colored heads instead of flat, metal ones because they are easier to grip and easier to spot on fabric and floors.

◆ **S A F E T Y P I N S :**

Some people are so resistant to basting their quilt layers together with thread that they use 1″ long rustproof safety pins, evenly spaced all over the quilt, and skip basting with thread entirely. (Note: It takes 350 to 500 safety pins to adequately secure the layers of a full-size bed quilt.)

The other advantage of safety-pin basting the quilt layers is that once the pins are closed, there are no sharp exposed points to prick your fingers. Many people feel, however, that thread-basting works much better than the safety-pin method of keeping the quilt layers from shifting, and it doesn't really take much longer.

Glue Sticks

Glue sticks can be used in appliqué for holding paper templates in place on fabric for marking, and for securing individual appliqués on background fabric for stitching.

Now that there are glue sticks made especially for fabrics, there is no need to use those made for paper (even if gluing paper templates to fabric). Fabric glue sticks contain an ingredient that helps them glide smoothly over fabric, but moisture (including humidity) and/or heat can make even a brand-new glue stick a gooey mess.

Store glue sticks in a cold, dry place when not in use. (Try keeping them in a sealed, air-tight container in your freezer.) Replace glue sticks if they become messy or difficult to work with.

Fusibles

Paper-backed fusible web, which is made of synthetic fibers, is very useful in preparing pieces for machine-appliqué and eliminates the need for pins. It makes fabric easier to cut and stabilizes the appliqué edges, preventing raveling and creating a crisp edge for satin-stitching.

Follow the manufacturer's directions to fuse lightweight web to the wrong side of the fabric. Mark and cut out the appliqués, then remove the paper backing and fuse the shapes to the background fabric.

Hoops and Frames

Wooden hoops or frames are often used to hold the quilt layers together, smoothly and with an even tautness, for hand-quilting. Hoops can also be used for free-machine quilting (see pages 229-233, "Quilting and Tufting"). The layers of a quilt should be basted together before insertion into a hoop or frame.

Some quilters prefer hoops because they are smaller and lighter in weight than frames, they take up less storage space, they are portable, and they allow the fabric to be retightened as needed. Hoops are more suitable for quilting individual blocks or wallhangings than for a completely assembled quilt.

◆ **H O O P S :**

Quilting hoops are generally sturdier than embroidery hoops and they are available in different shapes, such as round, oval, square, or rectangular. Semicircular hoops are also available, which are good for stitching borders or other areas close to a quilt's edges.

Hoops come in all sizes, but a diameter of 10″ to 20″ should handle most quilting needs. Some hoops have a detachable floor stand that frees the hands for stitching and permits the hoop to be tilted and/or raised for more comfortable quilting.

◆ **F R A M E S :**

Most quilting frames are rectangular and made of wood, consisting of one or two pairs of top rails (the frame) supported by sturdy legs.

Frames come in a wide range of sizes (30″ to 120″) to accommodate any quilt up to king-size. The quilt edges are pinned or stitched flat to the rails, to smooth, straighten, and secure the layers. One or both pairs of frame rails can be rotated to roll up the quilt and facilitate working on any area of it.

FOR STITCHING

Whether you stitch by hand or machine when making a quilt, your needles should be sharp, straight, and rustproof. If any of the quiltmaking will be done on a sewing machine, your machine should be checked (and oiled if necessary) to make sure it is in good working condition before you begin your quilting project.

Hand-Stitching

If moving the needle through the fabric is more of a struggle than a pleasure for you, it is probably because the soothing rhythm that makes hand-sewing enjoyable has been disrupted by the tools you are using.

Check your needle: Has it become too dull to slide easily through the fabric? Check your thimble: Does it fit properly? Does it have grooves or ridges to help push the needle along?

◆ **N E E D L E S :**

Needles for hand-sewing come in different sizes with varying degrees of tapering at the point. The higher the number of the needle, the shorter and finer the shaft. Needles called "sharps" are longer and more tapered than "betweens," which are relatively short and stubby.

Buy an assortment of needles and try several different sizes for each application, then stick with the needles that seem to work best for you. For piecing and basting the quilt layers together, try #7 or #8 sharps. For appliqué try #7 to #12 sharps. For hand-quilting try #7 to #10 betweens.

◆ **T H I M B L E S :**

Few people enjoy using a thimble for hand-sewing, but most use one anyway because they find it preferable to sore and bleeding fingers. Thimbles come in sizes, so experiment to find one that fits.

Metal thimbles (with dimples and/or ridges) are the most common type used and they also provide the most protection to fingers. Wear a metal thimble on your middle finger and use it to push the needle, leaving your index finger and thumb free to pull or insert it.

Leather thimbles are softer than metal ones (and supple, too) and they allow fingers to "breathe," but their relative softness makes them generally less protective. There are leather thimbles with metal tips that can be an acceptable compromise.

Machine-Stitching

For piecing or quilting, almost any straight-stitch sewing machine will suffice, so long as it is in good working condition and makes straight rows of even stitching (backstitching, too, if you want to use it for anchoring seam ends). For appliqué the machine must be able to satin-stitch (closely spaced zigzag stitches) as well, and decorative machine stitches might also be desirable.

Using the appropriate needle and presser foot for each sewing application will make machine-stitching go a lot faster with a minimum of frustration.

◆ **NEEDLES:** Needles for machine-stitching come in a variety of sizes with one of several different shapes at the point. Start each quilting project with an adequate supply of new needles, because those that bend or break during stitching will have to be replaced immediately. "Jeans" needles have sharp points that can go through fabric by piercing the threads, making perfectly straight stitching lines.

Ballpoint or semi-ballpoint needles cannot pierce thread, so they go through fabric by spreading the threads and sliding between them. Although this type of needle is preferred for most machine-stitching applications, going only in the spaces between the fabric threads can lead to stitching lines that are not truly straight.

For piecing, a #11 needle should give good results. For appliqué (satin stitch), try a #10 or #11 needle. For quilting, try a #14 needle. Also check the manual that came with your sewing machine for the manufacturer's suggestions about needles.

PRESSER FEET
◆ **STRAIGHT-STITCH FOOT:**
Used for piecing and quilting. A straight-stitch foot, which has a straight, narrow slit along its center and can often double as a ¼" seam guide, is standard equipment on most sewing machines.
◆ **EVEN-FEED (WALKING) FOOT:**
Used for quilting or binding. An even-feed foot keeps the fabric layers from shifting as they pass through the machine.
◆ **DARNING FOOT:**
Used for free-machine quilting. A darning foot, which is used whenever the feed dogs are lowered, has a light touch and prevents the skipped stitches than can occur during free-machine quilting when no presser foot at all is used.
◆ **APPLIQUÉ (ZIGZAG) FOOT:**
Used for appliqué. An appliqué foot can also be used whenever a wide view of the stitching line is desired.

SEAM GAUGE
If fabric pieces have no seam lines marked on them, you need an accurate way of stitching the ¼" seams that patchwork requires. Sewing machines usually come with at least one seam gauge, and gauges of various types are also available in fabric stores.

One type of ready-made seam gauge is a metal (or plastic) plate adjacent to, or part of, the straight-stitch throat plate, which has ⅛" or ¼" increments premarked on it. Another type is a straight-edge attachment whose distance from the needle is adjustable. A tightening screw usually secures this type of gauge.

If you don't have a seam gauge, you can make one: Place a strip of drafting, masking, or quilting tape on the throat plate exactly ¼" from the needle as a guide.

SEAM RIPPERS
If machine-stitches must be removed (accidents happen!), a seam ripper will do the job better than any other tool. The longer of its two pointed tips can be inserted under the loop of an individual stitch to cut it, and the sharp blade can be slipped along the seam between fabric pieces (with seam allowances spread open) to quickly remove an entire line of stitching. (Note: Never use a single-edge razor blade instead of a seam ripper.)

FOR PRESSING

The basics for pressing (or ironing) are a steam iron and an ironing board. A full-size iron works just fine, but a smaller, travel-size iron with a pointy tip can be handy for pressing small pieces of fabric and sharp points. Make sure the plate on the bottom of the iron is clean, to prevent staining fabric.

The ironing board should be at a comfortable height for you, and the cover should be laundered or replaced as needed to avoid stains on your project. Many quilters like to place a padded table adjacent to their sewing machines so they can stitch and press without getting up.

SOME OTHER HELPFUL GADGETS
◆ **BIAS STRIP FOLDING TOOL:**
Used for folding under the long edges of a bias strip for appliqué. They come in several sizes for making different size strips. (Optional: You can get the same results with two straight pins anchored to an ironing board.)
◆ **BIAS TUBE PRESSING GUIDES:**
Used for pressing under the seam allowance of a bias tube (a bias strip folded in half and stitched right side out). This is a speedy method of preparing bias strips for appliquéd stems, vines, or other sinuous designs.

Fabric and Thread

Although selecting fabric and thread for a quilting project is mainly a matter of personal preference, this section presents some guidelines to help in making your choices. When designing your own quilt, the time spent laying out sample arrangements of colors and/or prints is very worthwhile. Experiment to your heart's content—many of the following rules were made to be broken!

FABRIC

Take into consideration the quilt's planned use. Fabrics for crib and bed quilts should be durable and able to withstand repeated washings, while decorative fabrics and those that require drycleaning are best reserved for wallhangings.

Fabrics used for the quilt top and backing should be similar in fiber content, weave, and weight.

Fiber Content, Weave, and Weight

Pure (100%) cotton is recommended for most quilting projects because it has the following properties:
- Wrinkle resistance
- Little or no shrinkage during washing
- Durability
- Tendency to take and hold creases well
- Ease in needling
- Evenness and firmness of weave

Cotton-polyester blends can also be used if they are at least 65% cotton. Keep in mind that polyester is resistant to creasing and is harder to needle than cotton, and it usually shrinks more than pure cotton does. Avoid mixing pure cotton and cotton blends. Use one or the other.

Choose fabrics of light or medium (broadcloth) weight which are neither too loosely nor too tightly woven. Avoid any fabric that feels stiff, stretchy, or slippery.

Finishes

Sizing can make new fabric feel stiff, but it usually washes out. If fabric is limp after prewashing, spray sizing or starch can add enough body for easy handling and piecing.

Fabrics that are pretreated to help prevent stains from setting can be used for quilting so long as they are not too stiff to needle easily.

Permanent press fabrics resist wrinkles, but they also resist creasing and cannot be permanently straightened by pulling on the bias because of the "memory" built into the fibers.

Some methods of applying prints to fabric can result in a stiffness or tightness of the weave which will not relax, even after prewashing, so check print fabrics carefully before purchasing.

Color and Design

Make a bed quilt or wallhanging in colors that coordinate with the room in which it will be used/displayed, or make it in colors that are pleasing to you or to the person who will receive it as a gift.

Use solids, prints, dots, or stripes. Experiment with different colors and combinations of colors, first with colored pencils and paper, then with fabric swatches (see "Making a Sample Block," later in this section).

The Color Wheel

The color wheel can help you understand why some colors work together while others seem to clash. Colors that sit adjacent to one another on the wheel will blend quietly; to enliven a color add one from the opposite side. All colors alter in appearance when placed next to different colors. Any color will gain importance as you add more of it to any arrangement.

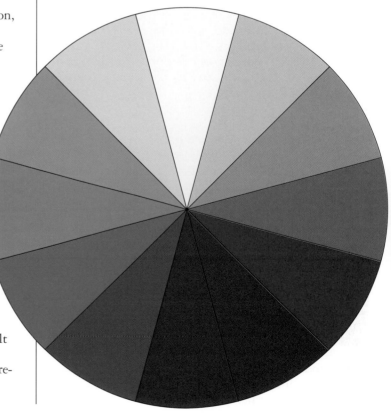

COLOR VOCABULARY

PRIMARY COLORS:
Yellow, red, blue

SECONDARY COLORS:
Orange, violet, green (halfway between primary colors on color wheel)

TERTIARY COLORS:
Yellow-orange, red-orange, red-violet, blue-violet, blue-green, yellow-green (between primary and secondary colors on wheel)

NEUTRAL TONES:
White, gray, black, beige

TINT:
Made by adding white to a color (e.g., pink is a tint of red)

SHADE:
Made by adding black to a color (e.g., maroon is a shade of red)

WARM COLORS:
Yellow, orange, red (visually stimulating)

COOL COLORS:
Violet, blue, green (visually soothing)

Color Schemes

Consider the value of colors (light, medium, or dark) when planning a color scheme. Dark colors seem brighter against a white or beige background. Against a black background, muted colors can have a somber look (as in Amish quilts), and bright, solid colors can appear to shine like stained glass.

Consider also the proportion and placement of the colors and prints, which will have an important effect on a quilt's overall look.

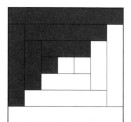
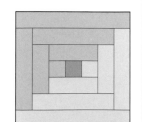

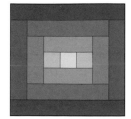

Mix and match color values based on the effect you want. Use high-contrast, solid colors for a bold look and low-contrast, soft prints for a quiet, subdued look.

Prints

Use dense, allover prints for small pieces, as these tend to get lost between the motifs of a sparse print and wind up looking like solids. Small, allover prints can also be used for backing, to camouflage seams and quilting lines.

Use large-scale prints for large pieces or to create different effects on small pieces.

Stripes

Stripes can be a striking addition to a quilt, but they require special care in cutting and extra fabric to allow for waste. You can use the stripes as guides for straight edges.

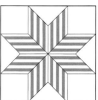
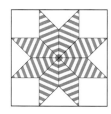

COLOR SCHEMES

ACHROMATIC:
Without color; neutral tones

MONOCHROMATIC:
Shades and/or tints of one color (e.g., pink, dusty rose, maroon)

POLYCHROMATIC:
Several colors, or shades and/or tints of several colors (e.g., salmon, light sea-green, light violet)

ANALOGOUS:
Two or more adjacent colors on color wheel (e.g., yellow, yellow-green, green)

COMPLEMENTARY:
Two opposite colors on wheel (e.g., red, green)

Making a Sample Block

Make a sample block to test each proposed color scheme. Many quilters pin sample blocks onto a plain fabric "wall" to test the effect of a color scheme over a large area, or even a whole quilt.

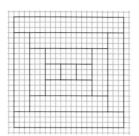

1. Draw a full-size, finished block on graph paper.

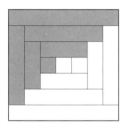
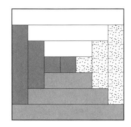
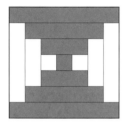
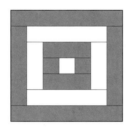

2. Cut enough fabric pieces (without seam allowance) to make sample block.

3. Use glue stick to glue fabric pieces to graph paper block like a jigsaw puzzle, butting edges.

Prewashing Fabric

Prewash fabrics before cutting, to remove sizing and excess dye, and to preshrink.

Unfold fabric to single thickness. Trim away a tiny ($\frac{1}{4}''$) triangle from each fabric corner, to reduce raveling. Machine-wash each fabric separately in warm water with detergent. Line-dry fabric or tumble-dry in machine set for warm or permanent press until fabric is just damp. Iron damp fabric until it is dry and wrinkle-free. (Optional: Use spray sizing or starch.) Fold fabric neatly for storage if it won't be used right away.

Storing Fabric

Store fabric neatly on shelves in a closet or in clear plastic boxes, arranged according to color.

Label each fabric with its width and yardage, and update the label whenever a piece of fabric is used.

THREADS

Use matching thread for seams and appliqués; matching, contrasting, or invisible thread for quilting. For machine-quilting, use bobbin thread to match backing.

Cut thread on the diagonal to enable the end to slip more easily through the eye of a needle (or use a threader).

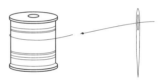

For hand-sewing, use 18" to 24" lengths of thread. Knot the cut end so that the thread will be drawn through the fabric in the same direction it came off the spool, to reduce fraying.

TYPES OF THREAD

PURE COTTON THREAD
Hand-piecing
Machine-piecing
Machine-quilting
Appliqué
QUILTING THREAD (WAXED OR UNWAXED)
Hand-quilting
INVISIBLE THREAD
Machine-quilting
EMBROIDERY THREAD
Embellishments
Decorative stitches for appliqué
Special quilting effects

The Quilt Components

By definition, a quilt contains three layers: a top, a backing, and a filler. In many cases the top is made up of several different components. If you stop to analyze what these are, how big they are, and how many of each you will need to make, you will get a good idea of the complexity of any given pattern before you begin to work—and you will also see ways to design your own variations.

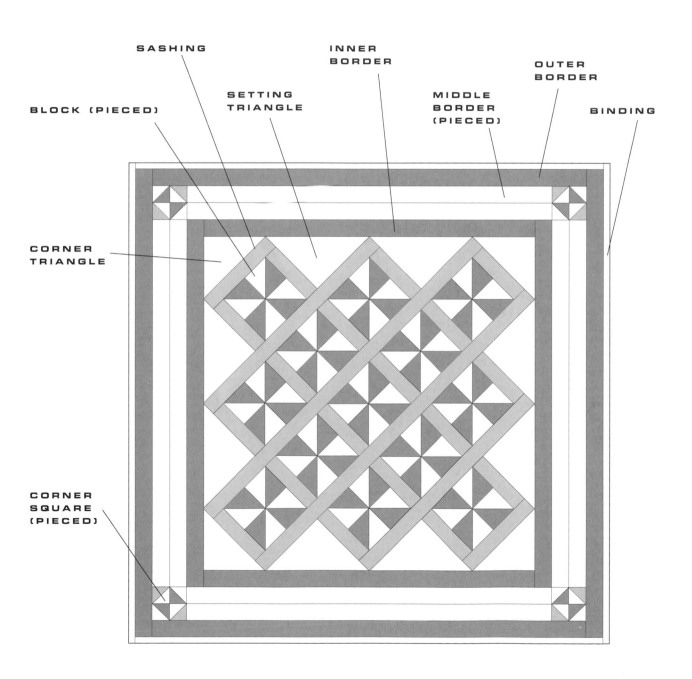

SASHING

INNER BORDER

OUTER BORDER

SETTING TRIANGLE

MIDDLE BORDER (PIECED)

BLOCK (PIECED)

BINDING

CORNER TRIANGLE

CORNER SQUARE (PIECED)

THE QUILT CENTER

The quilt center is made up of smaller components (plain or pieced, appliquéd or not), including one or more blocks and optional setting triangles, corner triangles, corner squares, and sashing.

Blocks

Pieced blocks are made up of smaller units, individual plain or pieced shapes that are assembled to make partial blocks and/or rows, which are then joined to complete the block.

4-PATCHES (2 X 2 UNITS)

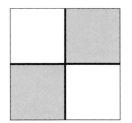 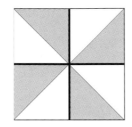 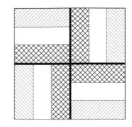 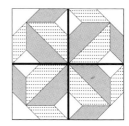

9-PATCHES (3 X 3 UNITS)

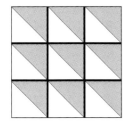 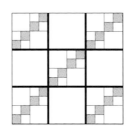 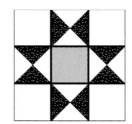 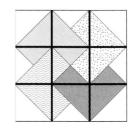

SOME OTHER CONFIGURATIONS

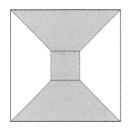 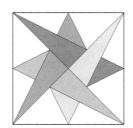 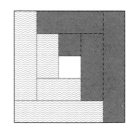 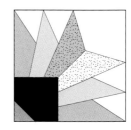

Sashing

Sashing separates or frames blocks. It enhances a quilt design and enlarges the quilt center (see pages 211-212, "Adjusting the Size").

   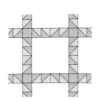 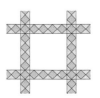

PLAIN
SASHING

PLAIN
SASHING WITH
PLAIN CORNER
SQUARES

PLAIN
SASHING WITH
PIECED CORNER
SQUARES

PIECED
SASHING WITH
PLAIN
CORNER
SQUARES

PIECED
SASHING WITH
MATCHING
CORNER
SQUARES

STRIP-PIECED
SASHING WITH
PIECED CORNER
SQUARES

Center Sets

The components of the quilt center can be arranged in straight, diagonal, or band sets.

STRAIGHT SETS

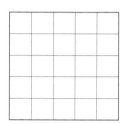

ONE BLOCK

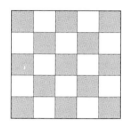

TWO BLOCKS

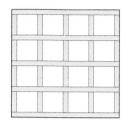

PLAIN SASHING

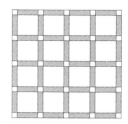

PLAIN SASHING
WITH CORNER
SQUARES

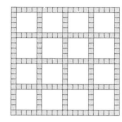

PIECED
SASHING

DIAGONAL SETS

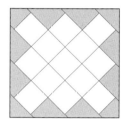

FLOATING THE
BLOCKS

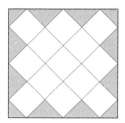

SETTING
TRIANGLES AND
CORNER
TRIANGLES

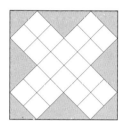

LARGE SETTING
TRIANGLES AND
CORNER
TRIANGLES

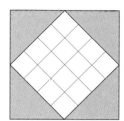

EXTRA-LARGE
CORNER
TRIANGLES

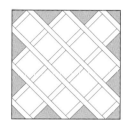

PLAIN SASHING
WITH SETTING
TRIANGLES AND
CORNER
TRIANGLES

BAND SETS

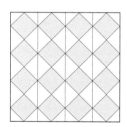

ON-POINT BLOCKS
AND HALF-BLOCKS

ZIGZAG BANDS OF
ON-POINT BLOCKS
AND HALF-BLOCKS

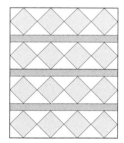

ON-POINT BLOCKS
WITH PLAIN
HORIZONTAL
SASHING

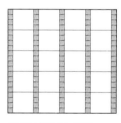

STRAIGHT-SET
BLOCKS WITH
PIECED VERTICAL
SASHING

BORDERS

Borders frame the quilt center. They can be plain or pieced, appliquéd or not, all the same or all different, and have square or mitered corners. Borders are added to the quilt one at a time, from the center out, with strips joined to one pair of opposite quilt edges first and then to the remaining pair. When using large-scale print fabrics, plan the placement of the motifs on the border to create attractive joinings at the corners.

PLAIN BORDER
WITH MITERED
CORNERS

PLAIN BORDER
WITH BUTTED
CORNERS

PLAIN BORDER
WITH PLAIN
CORNER
SQUARES

PLAIN BORDER
WITH PIECED
CORNER
SQUARES

STRIP-PIECED
BORDER WITH
PIECED CORNER
SQUARES

PIECED DIREC-
TIONAL BORDER
WITH PIECED
CORNER
SQUARES

Spacer Borders

Spacer borders enlarge the size of a quilt more in one direction than the other. They can be added in single pairs (either horizontal or vertical) or in two pairs (both horizontal and vertical), with one pair wider than the other.

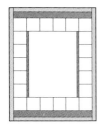 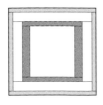

TWO 2-STRIP SPACER BORDERS

ONE 4-STRIP SPACER BORDER

Mitered Corners

Mitered corner seams are stitched by hand or by machine, as directed below, after all the border strips have been machine-stitched to the quilt center. For multiple borders, the strips for an individual quilt edge are joined together to form a strip set, which is then treated as a single border strip.

Border strip length = Length of quilt edge + (Border strip width x 2)

HAND-STITCHED MITER

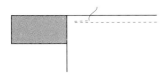

1. Stitch each border strip to quilt, beginning and ending ¼" from quilt ends; secure with backstitching.

2. Place quilt flat, right side up, lapping border strip ends.

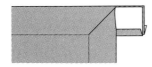

3. At one corner, press under the upper strip end on a 45° angle. Slipstitch folded edge to strip underneath. Press. Trim excess fabric.

MACHINE-STITCHED MITER

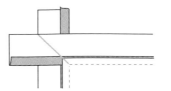 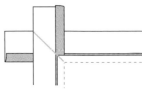

1. Stitch border strips to quilt in same manner as for hand-stitched miter, Step 1. Place quilt flat, wrong side up, lapping border strip ends.

2. At one corner, mark a 45° diagonal on the upper strip end. Reverse lapping to mark underneath strip.

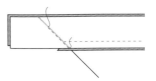

3. Fold quilt corner on the diagonal, right sides together, with edges even and seam allowances pressed away from border. Align and pin together marked lines on border strips. Stitch on one marked line, beginning at inner border corner. Press. Trim excess fabric.

BATTING

Batting is the soft layer between the quilt top and backing which gives dimension to the quilt and definition to the quilted designs. It comes in various thicknesses (¼" to 3") and fibers (wool, silk, cotton, cotton/polyester, and 100% polyester), and is available by the yard (45", 48", 60", and 90" wide) and packaged to fit standard bed sizes.

Batting is often bonded, glazed, or needle-punched, which helps to reduce bearding (the migration of the fibers outward through the fabric layers, mostly during quilting or washing) but may also create surfaces that are harder to needle than other types of batting.

Bonded polyester, cotton, and cotton/polyester type battings are generally preferred for most quilting projects. The low-loft type is best for thin quilts with closely spaced lines of hand-quilting. The high-loft type is best in tufted comforters and for quilts with large, machine-quilted outlines. Batting of medium thickness is often called all-purpose.

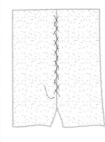

PACKAGED BATTING SIZES	
Crib	45" x 60"
Twin	72" x 90"
Full	81" x 96"
Queen	90" x 108"
	90" x 120"
King	120" x 120"

Batting should be at least 3″ to 4″ larger than the quilt top on all sides and trimmed to size after quilting. It can be a single panel or pieced by hand with wide catch-stitches.

BACKING

Backing can be a single fabric panel or pieced, cut from one or more fabrics, ordinary in appearance or as decorative as the quilt top. It should be at least 3″ to 4″ larger than the quilt top on all sides and trimmed to size after quilting.

BINDING

Binding protects the quilt edges. It can be self-finishing (folding and stitching either the quilt front or the backing over the raw edge to bind the quilt, or by turning front and back edges to the inside and stitching them together along the folds), or it can consist of one or more separate strips. Binding strips can be cut on either the straight grain or the bias, but unless the quilt edges are curved, there's no need to use bias binding.

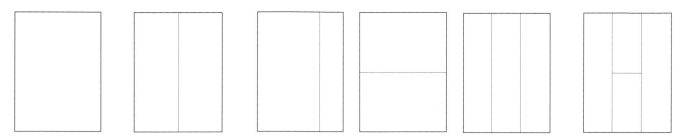

Adjusting the Size

You can alter the final dimensions of almost any quilt by adding or omitting blocks, sashing, or borders; by changing the way you arrange these components; or by enlarging or reducing their size.

BED QUILT AND WALLHANGING SIZES

The size a quilt should be depends on its intended use. A wallhanging can be as small as a place mat, large enough to cover an entire wall, or any size in between. For a bed quilt, the size is calculated as follows:

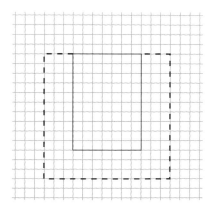

1. Draw mattress shape on graph paper. Add length of drop (8″ to 14″ for coverlet, 21″ or measured length for bedspread) at sides and bottom.

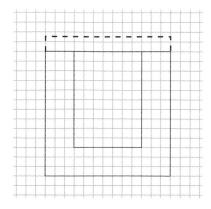

2. Add pillow tuck (8″ to 12″) at top, if desired.

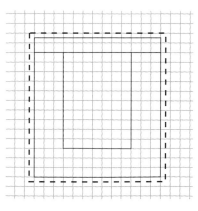

3. Add 2″ to 4″ at all four sides, to allow for shrinkage during quilting. Resulting outline is design size of quilt top. Finished size will be slightly smaller.

MATTRESS AND SAMPLE FINISHED BED QUILT SIZES

BED	MATTRESS	COVERLET*	BEDSPREAD**
Crib	27″ × 52″	40″ × 60″	
Twin	39″ × 74″	65″ × 98″	81″ × 106″
Full	54″ × 74″	80″ × 98″	96″ × 106″
Queen	60″ × 80″	86″ × 104″	102″ × 112″
King	76″ × 80″	102″ × 104″	118″ × 112″

*Based on 13″ drop and 11″ pillow tuck, for all except crib.
**Based on 21″ drop and 11″ pillow tuck.

Ways to Change the Size

Adjust the given size in individual quilt instructions for either a wallhanging or bed quilt by making one or more of the following changes to the quilt top.

CHANGE THE NUMBER OF BLOCKS

9 BLOCKS

16 BLOCKS

20 BLOCKS

CHANGE THE LAYOUT OF THE BLOCKS

STRAIGHT SET

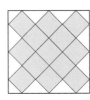

DIAGONAL SET

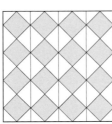

BAND SET

CHANGE THE WIDTH OF THE SASHING STRIPS

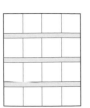

2″-WIDE STRIPS

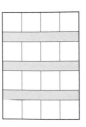

4″-WIDE STRIPS

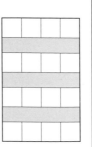

6″-WIDE STRIPS

CHANGE THE SIZE OF THE BLOCKS

8″ BLOCK

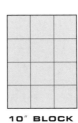

10″ BLOCK

12″ BLOCK

CHANGE THE NUMBER OF SASHING STRIPS

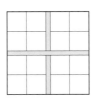

2 STRIPS

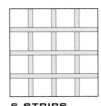

6 STRIPS

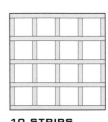

10 STRIPS

CHANGE THE NUMBER AND/OR WIDTH OF THE BORDERS

2 BORDERS

3 BORDERS

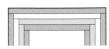

4 BORDERS

1 WIDE BORDER

WIDER MIDDLE BORDER

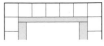

INNER SPACER BORDER

212

Determining Fabric Quantities

If you are designing your own quilt, or the pattern you have does not provide them, you can figure yardage requirements by spending a little time and using some basic math. It's really easier than you might expect.

QUILT TOP

Draw the quilt top on graph paper. Draw the pieces on one of each different block and identify the unmarked blocks. Mark the finished dimensions of each unit, and add coloring or shading to identify different fabrics.

Make a chart listing the cut size of each component and the number needed, grouping pieces according to fabric. (To calculate cut size and pair pieces for efficient layout, see page 215.)

Round off numbers for easier calculating. Next, make a separate cutting layout for each fabric, planning the largest pieces before smaller ones. (The longest strips frequently determine the amount of fabric needed.) Figure on a usable width of 40" for 44"/45" wide fabric, to allow for selvages and preshrinking. The following illustrations are an example of how to determine yardage this way.

SAMPLE QUILT TOP DRAWING

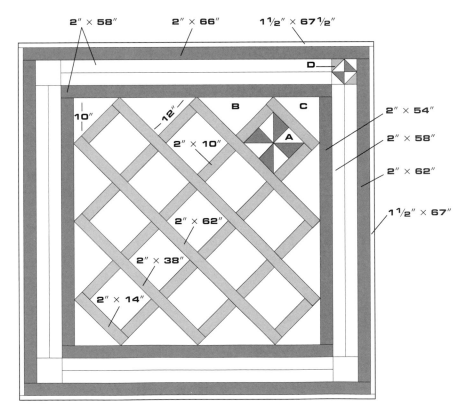

SAMPLE CHART

PIECE	SIZE	NUMBER	AREA	YARDAGE
A	2⅞" × 2⅞"	26	12" × 20"	3 yds. White
B	12⅞" × 12⅞"	4	26" × 26"	
C	10⅞" × 10⅞"	2	11" × 22"	
D	1⅞" × 1⅞"	8	4" × 8"	
Second Border*	2½" × 62½"	8	20" × 63"	
Binding	2" × 72"	4	8" × 72"	
D	1⅞" × 1⅞"	4	2" × 8"	2 yds. Red
Sashing*	2½" × 14½"	18	13" × 58"	
	2½" × 18½"	2	3" × 37"	
	2½" × 42½"	2	5" × 43"	
	2½" × 66½"	2	5" × 67"	
A	2⅞" × 2⅞"	26	12" × 20"	2 yds. Blue
D	1⅞" × 1⅞"	4	2" × 8"	
First Border*	2½" × 58½"	2	5" × 59"	
	2½" × 62½"	2	5" × 63"	
Third Border*	2½" × 66½"	2	5" × 67"	
	2½" × 70½"	2	5" × 71"	

*Extra length included.

SAMPLE CUTTING LAYOUTS

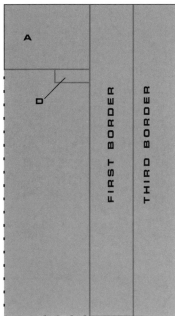

2 YDS. BLUE

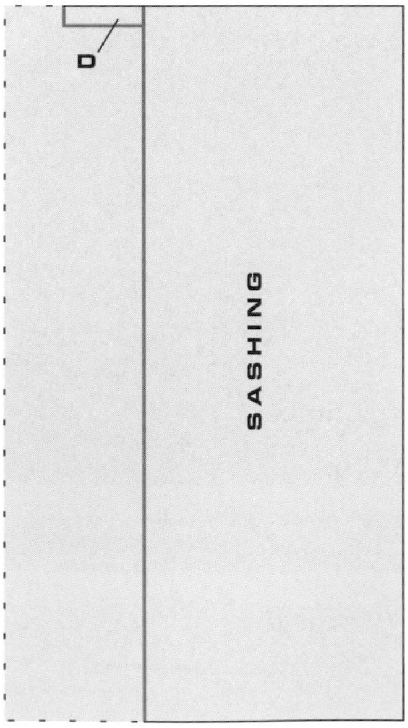

1¾ YDS. RED

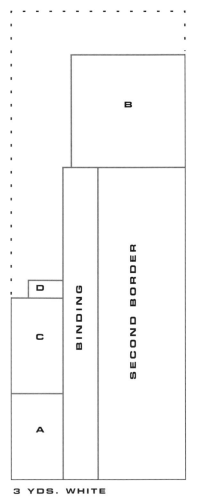

3 YDS. WHITE

DETERMINING PIECE DIMENSIONS

1. Determine cut size of each piece, including seam allowance.

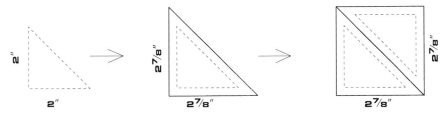

◆ **For square and rectangular pieces:** *Allow for ¼" seams by adding ½" to each finished edge.*

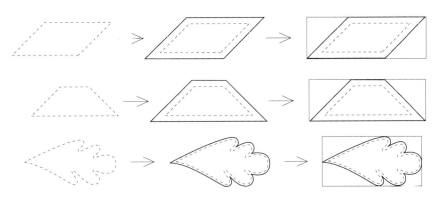

◆ **For right triangles:** *Allow for ¼" seams by adding ⅞" to short edges and 1¼" to long edge. For easier calculating, pair two triangles to form a square.*

◆ *For equilateral triangles, parallelograms, trapezoids, curves, and other nonsquare shapes: Add ¼" seam allowance (⅛" to ¼" for appliqués) and draw a square or rectangle around the shape.*

◆ *For sashing: Allow for ¼" seams by adding ½" to strip width. Calculate length across rows of blocks and block-length sashing.*

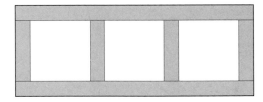

Sashing strip length = (Finished block side × Number of blocks across row)
  + (Finished sashing width × Number of sashing strips)
  + 4"

◆ *For borders: Allow for ¼" seams by adding ½" to strip width.*
◆ *For borders with mitered corners:*
  Border length = Finished border length + (Finished border width × 2) + 4"
◆ *For borders with butted corners:*
  Border length = Finished border length + 4"

2. Determine how many of each piece are needed.
◆ *For block pieces:*
  Number of each piece needed = Number of pieces per block × Number of blocks

3. Determine fabric area needed.

Fabric area = Piece length × Piece width × Number of pieces

◆ For bias strips cut from a fabric square:

Sides of square = $\sqrt{\text{Bias strip length} \times \text{Bias strip width}}$

Example:

Bias strip length = 640″
Bias strip width = 2½″
Sides of square = $\sqrt{640″ \times 2½″}$
Sides of square = $\sqrt{1296 \text{ sq. in.}}$
Sides of square = 36″

4. Determine yardage needed. Draw a cutting layout on graph paper based on your calculations. If all pieces to be cut are the same size, use the following equation (40 equals usable fabric width, and 36 equals number of inches in a yard).

Yardage = (Number of pieces ÷ (40 ÷ Piece length)) × (Piece width ÷ 36)

BACKING AND BATTING

Backing/batting yardage = (Quilt top length + 8″) × Number of panels ÷ 36

SAMPLE BACKING/BATTING YARDAGES*		
	COVERLET	**BEDSPREAD**
Crib	1 ¾ yds.	
Twin	6 yds.	6½ yds.
Full	6 yds.	9½ yds.
Queen	9 yds.	9½ yds.
King	9½ yds.	10 yds.
* Or use packaged batting (see pages 207-211, "The Quilt Components," for sizes).		

BINDING

Binding strip length = Perimeter of quilt + 15″
Fabric area = Binding strip length × Binding strip width
Sides of square for cutting bias binding = $\sqrt{\text{Fabric area}}$
Yardage = Fabric area ÷ 1440 sq. in.

In the preceding equation 1440 equals 40 × 36, the number of usable square inches in one yard of fabric.

Preparing Patterns and Templates

Although rotary cutters and transparent rulers allow you to cut almost any piece you need without first making templates and marking their outlines onto your fabric, you may need (or want) to use sturdy patterns to mark appliqué pieces or quilting designs, or to take advantage of specific motifs on printed fabric.

PREPARING PATTERNS

Enlarge, complete, or draft patterns as directed below, adding ¼″ seam allowance as needed. Trace full-size patterns provided in individual project directions, or photocopy them on a high-quality copy machine. Make templates (later in this section) from full-size, complete patterns.

Enlarging Patterns on a Grid

Have patterns enlarged on a professional copy machine, or transpose them by hand to a full-size grid drawn on graph paper (see individual project directions for size of grid squares).

1. Mark same number of rows and columns of grid squares on graph paper as on original grid.

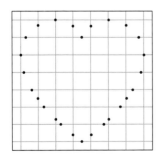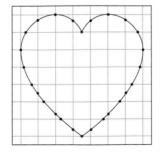

2. On full-size grid, mark where pattern lines intersect grid lines. Connect markings.

Completing Half- and Quarter-Patterns

A half- or quarter-pattern can be reversed, flopped, and/or rotated on fabric to mark a complete shape, or the partial pattern can be completed before marking fabric.

◆ *For half-patterns: Make two tracings of original pattern. Reverse one tracing and tape both together, matching the center markings.*

◆ *For quarter-patterns: Tape two tracings together to make a half-pattern. Make a tracing of half-pattern, reverse one half-pattern, and tape both halves together.*

Drafting Patterns from Dimensions

If project directions provide dimensions instead of patterns, draft full-size patterns on graph paper, taping sheets of paper together as necessary for large patterns.

FRACTION	¹⁄₁₆	⅛	³⁄₁₆	¼	⁵⁄₁₆	⅜	⁷⁄₁₆	½	⁹⁄₁₆	⅝	¹¹⁄₁₆	¾	¹³⁄₁₆	⅞	¹⁵⁄₁₆
DECIMAL	.0625	.125	.1875	.25	.3125	.375	.4375	.5	.5625	.625	.6875	.75	.8125	.875	.9375

Right Triangles

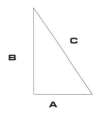

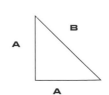

$$A^2 + B^2 = C^2$$

$$C = \sqrt{A^2 + B^2}$$

$$B^2 = 2A^2$$
$$B = A \times 1.41$$
$$A = B \times .707$$

Equilateral Triangles

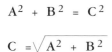

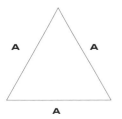

$$B^2 = A^2 - (\tfrac{1}{2}A)^2$$
$$B = .89A$$

Circles

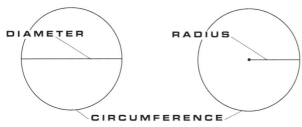

Radius = Diameter ÷ 2
Circumference = Radius × 6.2834

Circle-Based Shapes

1. Draw a circle with compass (radius) set to finished length of one side of shape. Walk compass around circle to mark off six equal sections.
2. Connect marks to draw shape.

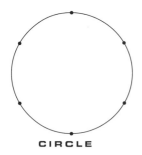

CIRCLE

HEXAGON

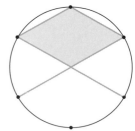

PARALLELOGRAM

Preparing Templates

Make a posterboard or Mylar template for each different full-size shape. Mark all templates with the project name, piece letter/name, and grain line. Label the right and wrong sides. Replace templates as they wear out.

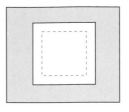

◆ *For posterboard templates:* Glue pattern, right side up, to posterboard. (Optional: Glue fine-grade sandpaper, rough side out, to opposite side of posterboard, to make a nonslip surface.)

◆ *For Mylar templates:* Use permanent marking pen to trace patterns on Mylar. Transfer all markings.

◆ *For hand-piecing and appliqué:* Cut out templates, with or without seam allowance, as you prefer (see pages 222-225).

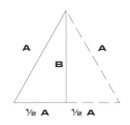

◆ *For machine-piecing:*
Cut out templates, including $\frac{1}{4}''$ seam allowance.

◆ *For window templates:* Make one continuous cut along seam line and another along cutting line. Use window templates for either hand- or machine-piecing.

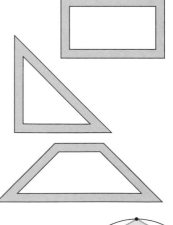

Marking and Cutting the Pieces

*E*xperienced quilters will tell you that the time spent cutting out pieces is time indeed—but careful cutting sets the stage for successful piecing, so it is time well spent. Use speed- and strip-cutting/piecing techniques whenever you can, and keep your cut-out pieces clean, organized, and labeled in food storage bags or large envelopes. While you should plan all your cuts before setting blade or scissors to cloth, you don't have to cut all the pieces for a large project at once. When working on a complex quilt, you might find it more enjoyable to cut and piece all of one set of components before beginning another.

PREPARING TO CUT

Plan the cuts before beginning. Fabric for the largest pieces, such as borders, should be marked first, then the smaller pieces for patchwork. (Note: Allow extra length for border pieces in case the actual quilt measurements differ from the planned size.)

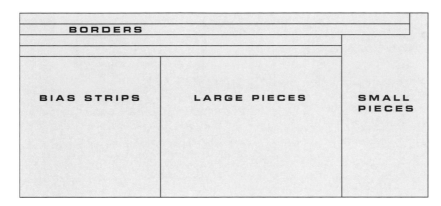

PLACEMENT ON THE FABRIC GRAIN

Cut the pieces with one or more long edges on the straight grain, parallel to the fabric threads. Cut as many pieces as possible on the crosswise grain to conserve fabric. Cut long pieces on the lengthwise grain to minimize piecing.

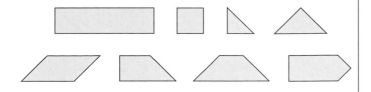

MARKING AND CUTTING WITH TEMPLATES

1. Position template, wrong side up, on wrong side of fabric, lining up template edges with fabric threads. (Turn template right side up for reverse pieces.) Leave at least ½" between pieces if templates do not include seam allowance; butt edges if they do.

2. Hold template firmly in place and mark around it with a sharp pencil (dark color pencil on light fabric; light color, white, or silver pencil on dark fabric). Apply only as much pressure on pencil as necessary, to avoid stretching fabric.

3. Cut pieces, including seam allowance, using scissors or rotary cutter.

SPEED CUTTING

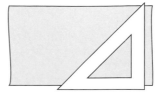

Line up a ruler or drafting triangle with the fabric threads, then use a rotary cutter to straighten edges and eliminate selvages before cutting individual pieces.

Cutting Units from Strips

1. Cut fabric into strips (see individual project directions for dimensions), including seam allowance in width of each.

2. For plain units, cut individual shapes from strips using quilter's ruler, drafting triangle, or other heavy, plastic template for accurate angles.

3. For strip-pieced units, stitch strips together lengthwise. Cut pieced units from resulting strip set. For bias squares and triangles, cut shapes on a 45° angle.

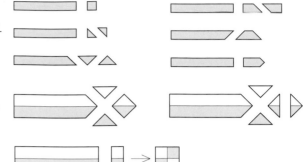

4. Stitch strip-pieced units together to form larger units or blocks.

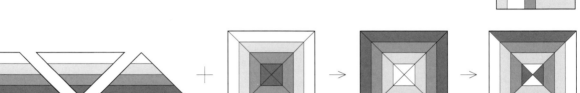

5. For Seminole patchwork, make strip sets, cut individual units, and join to form bands.

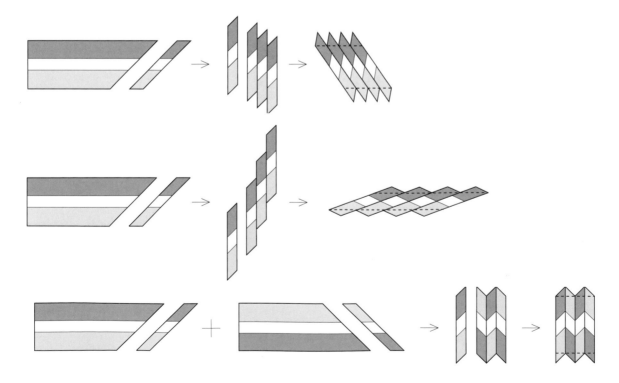

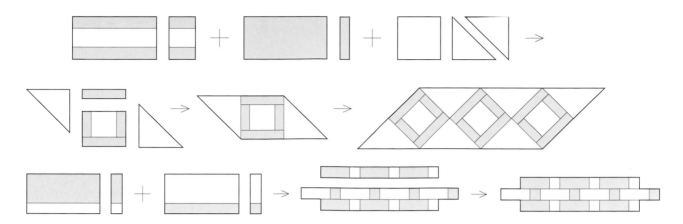

Speedy Triangle Squares

1. Cut matching pieces of two contrasting fabrics (see individual project directions for dimensions).

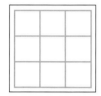 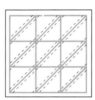

2. Mark a square grid on wrong side of lighter-color fabric, leaving ¹/₂″ margin all around grid. Mark half as many grid squares as triangle squares (or triangle-triangle squares) needed; each marked square will make two pieced squares. (Note: Mark grid squares ⁷/₈″ larger than desired finished size of triangle squares or 1¹/₄″ larger than desired finished size of Speedy Triangle-Triangle Squares, below.)

3. Mark diagonals across squares.

4. Pin marked fabric to contrasting fabric, right sides together. Stitch ¹/₄″ from each diagonal, on both sides of line.

5. Cut along marked lines, grid lines first and then diagonals.

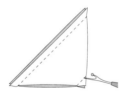

6. Remove corner stitches.

7. Open triangles. Press seams toward darker fabric.

Speedy Triangle-Triangle Squares

 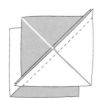

1. Make Speedy Triangle Squares, above. Mark the diagonal on wrong side of one Speedy Triangle Square.

2. Pin marked square to a matching unmarked one, right sides together, with contrasting halves facing, aligning seams and edges.

3. Stitch ¹/₄″ from marked diagonal, on both sides of line.

4. Cut along marked line. Open triangles. Press.

Stitching and Pressing the Pieces

As quick and efficient as quiltmaking can be with a sewing machine, many people still prefer the look of handmade quilts and find handwork relaxing and enjoyable, so both hand- and machine-piecing techniques are covered in this chapter.

HAND PIECING

Patchwork can be assembled by hand with straight stitching (running stitch, backstitch, or a combination of the two) or whipstitching (also called English paper-piecing). Hand-stitching is also useful for curved edges and set-in pieces.

Pinning pieces together before hand-stitching straight edges is optional. Some quilters only pin the ends of seams, others use so many pins that it's hard to see where to stitch, and still others never pin at all, except when working with slippery fabrics.

Anchor thread at the beginning and end of hand-sewn seams with two or three tiny backstitches; do not make knots.

Straight Seams

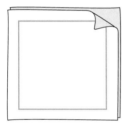

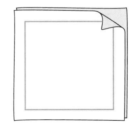

1. Cut out fabric pieces for hand-stitching (pages 219-221, "Marking and Cutting the Pieces"). Place two fabric pieces together, wrong sides out.

2. Put a pin through both fabric layers at ends of seam line to be stitched; align marked seam lines and secure pins. Add more pins as needed.

3. Make tiny (10 to 16 per inch) running stitches or backstitches along seam lines; do not stitch into seam allowance.

STRAIGHT STITCHES FOR HAND-PIECING

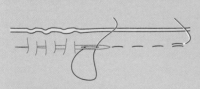

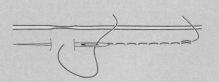

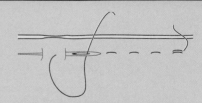

RUNNING STITCH
Make evenly spaced stitches (they should look the same on both sides of the fabric). Load the needle with as many stitches at one time as possible to minimize the number of long pulls of thread through the fabric, thereby saving time and energy.

BACKSTITCH
Backstitching uses three times as much thread as running stitches, and the number of long pulls of thread through the fabric is equal to the number of individual stitches (which requires more time and energy than for running stitches), but backstitching makes a sturdier seam.

ANCHORED RUNNING STITCH
Make running stitches, anchoring the thread with a backstitch immediately after each long pull of thread through the fabric.

Whipstitched Edges (English Paper-Piecing)

This technique creates crisp edges and points, and is useful for nonrectilinear shapes, such as parallelograms, trapezoids, and hexagons, as well as for set-in pieces. Another advantage of paper-piecing is that accurately prepared fabric edges will match up perfectly because the seam allowance is folded under before stitching. However, because there is no free seam allowance to press to one side after stitching, the patchwork won't be as sturdy as it might be if it had straight-stitched pieces.

PREPARING THE PIECES

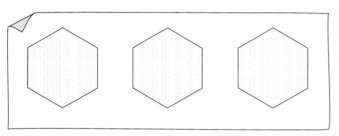

1. Make a freezer paper template for each fabric piece needed, omitting seam allowance (see pages 217-218, "Preparing Patterns and Templates"). Arrange paper shapes, shiny side down, on wrong side of fabric, leaving at least ½" around each template (more for acute angles). Fuse templates to fabric, using dry iron on wool setting.

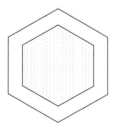 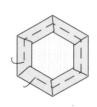

2. Cut out individual shapes from fabric, adding ½" seam allowance around each paper template.

3. Fold and press seam allowance smoothly over template edges without folding or creasing paper; baste in place halfway between raw fabric edge and outer fold.

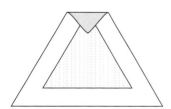 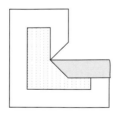

◆ *For acute outer corners (less than 90°): Fold down fabric point before folding adjacent edges.*

◆ *For inner corners: Clip into seam allowance at corner before folding.*

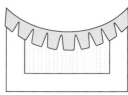 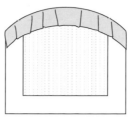

◆ *For outer curves: Make tucks as needed so that folded edges lie flat.*

◆ *For inner curves: Clip into seam allowance as needed so that folded edges lie flat.*

JOINING THE PIECES

1. Place two fabric pieces together, wrong sides out, aligning edges to be joined.
2. Whipstitch fabric edges, making tiny stitches (1/16" to 1/8" apart), being careful not to catch paper templates in stitches.
3. After all edges of a fabric piece have been stitched, carefully remove basting and paper.
(Note: Templates that have not been creased, folded, or torn can be reused to prepare additional fabric shapes.)

MACHINE PIECING

Pinning pieces together before machine-stitching straight edges is optional, as is anchoring thread at the beginning and end of machine-stitched seams. If the sewing machine is set for medium-to-small stitches (12 to 15 per inch), it usually isn't necessary to backstitch at each end of a seam, although some quilters prefer to secure their seam ends anyway. If your stitches are small and tight enough to hold without backstitching, you can save time by omitting the anchoring stitches. Most pieces cut for machine-stitching have no seam lines marked, so it is important to use an accurate gauge to make sure seams are exactly ¼" from fabric edges (see pages 198-203, "Tools and Equipment").

Test the Accuracy of Your Seam Gauge

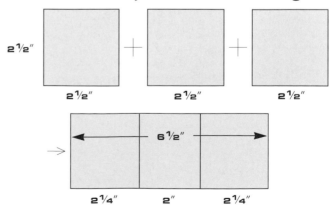

1. Machine-piece three 2½" fabric squares as directed opposite for straight seams, to form a strip.
2. Press strip. Measure length from end to end.
3. If strip is not exactly 6½" long, adjust gauge and repeat test.

Straight Seams

START

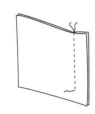

FINISH

1. Cut out fabric pieces for machine-stitching (see pages 219-221, "Marking and Cutting the Pieces").
2. Place two fabric pieces together, wrong sides out, aligning edges to be joined.
3. Stitch ¼″ seam from one end of piece to the other.

◆ **For acute angles (less than 90°):** *Start at end with larger corner angle and stitch across piece to end with acute angle. (Note: Stitching into seam allowance is not advisable at acute angles. Unless the seam allowance is left free, it may be difficult to align adjacent edges that have not yet been stitched.)*

ASSEMBLY-LINE STITCHING

To speed up machine-piecing, like pairs of fabric edges can be joined at the same time with a single line of stitches, which requires that the pieces be organized before you sit down at the sewing machine to stitch them.

Assembly-line stitching (also called chain-stitching) can be used to join individual pieces into a block or to join the blocks themselves.

ORGANIZING THE PIECES

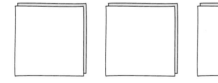

1. Place together pairs of fabric pieces, wrong sides out, aligning edges to be joined.
2. Stack pairs on top of each other with like edges aligned.
3. Place stack on sewing machine table with fabric edges to be stitched on the right-hand side, facing the proper direction for feeding through the machine.

STITCHING THE PIECES

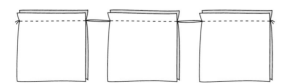

1. Machine-stitch first pair of pieces as usual; do not break threads after stitching across fabric.
2. Stitch about ½″ beyond fabric, forming a thread chain; stop with needle up.
3. Lift presser foot. Position second pair of pieces; lower needle and presser foot. Stitch in same manner as for first pair.
4. Continue joining pieces. Break threads after desired number of pieces have been joined.
5. Clip threads between pieces to cut shapes apart.

SET-IN PIECES

If two or more fabric pieces form an inside corner when they are joined, the piece that fits into the corner must be set-in and stitched, either by hand or machine, one seam at a time.

Set-in corners are stitched only along the seam line, not fabric edge to fabric edge, to leave the corner seam allowance free to be aligned with adjacent edges. Seam lines must meet exactly at the inner corner, so the seam lines should be marked.

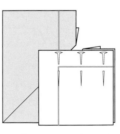 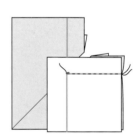

1. Place piece to be set-in against one outer piece, wrong sides out. Put a pin through both fabric layers at ends of seam line to be stitched; align marked seam lines and secure with pins.

2. Stitch (by hand or machine) along seam line, from inner corner outward, securing at inner corner with backstitching.

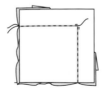

3. Align next pair of edges, keeping excess fabric out of the way. Stitch together as for first pair.

◆ **For multiple inner corners:** *Stitch one seam at a time, beginning at innermost seam(s) and working outward.*

CURVED SEAMS

Curved edges should always have their seam lines marked. If stitching by machine, stay-stitch concave seam lines before clipping or pinning.

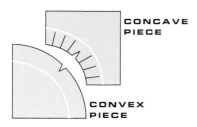

CONCAVE PIECE

CONVEX PIECE

1. Cut a ⅛″ deep V-shaped notch in center of both curved edges to be joined. Clip into seam allowance of concave (inner) curve as needed, up to but not into or beyond seam lines. Do not clip convex (outer) edge.

2. Place pieces together, wrong sides out, aligning center notches. Pin at notches, seam ends, and in between, stretching and/or easing edges as needed to align.

3. Hand- or machine-stitch, making ¼″ seam.

PRESSING

Ironing is done to remove wrinkles after prewashing fabric but before marking and cutting, by sliding the iron back and forth across the fabric.

Pressing is done to make seams lie flat by setting down the iron, applying momentary pressure, and then lifting the iron straight up and moving it to another area or seam and repeating. Patchwork is generally pressed (1) after each seam is stitched but before crossing it with another seam, (2) after individual blocks are completed, (3) after blocks are joined, and (4) after the entire quilt top is completed.

For most patchwork, seam allowances are pressed to one side for increased strength. Where pressing to one side would create bulk (such as at points where many pieces meet), the seams can be pressed open.

Fabric can be ironed or pressed on either side, but if done on the right side, you might want to use a press cloth to prevent glazing (shininess).

Press seams toward darker fabric whenever possible.

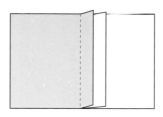

◆ *For seams pressed toward lighter fabric:* Trim darker seam allowance to ⅛″, to prevent it from extending beyond lighter seam allowance and showing through on right side.

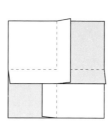 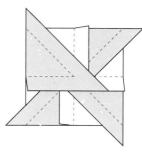

◆ *For intersections of seams:* Press seams away from each other, either open or to one side. (Note: At intersections of four or more pieces, press all seams either clockwise or counterclockwise.)

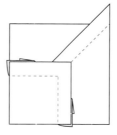 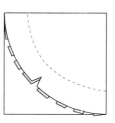

◆ *For set-in seams:* Press the joining seam(s) of the outer pieces to one side. Press seam allowances of the set-in piece flat, toward the outer pieces.

◆ *For curved seams:* Press toward concave edge.

Quilting Styles

Quilting designs can be obvious or subtle, plain or fancy, confined to a few individual areas of the quilt or stitched all over. The stitched patterns are more prominent on solid fabrics than on prints, and widely spaced lines of stitches create more depth of design than closely spaced ones. Closely spaced or allover quilting patterns are most successful when a thin, rather than puffy, batting is used.

OUTLINE QUILTING

Outline quilting repeats and/or emphasizes fabric shapes and can be done around patchwork or appliqué edges in one or more rows of stitching. Outline quilting can be used as an accent on any patch, block, or strip.

In-the-Ditch

Quilting in-the-ditch is a single line of stitching that is done right on the seam line around patches, along sashing and borders, or just outside the edge of an appliqué. It is usually done by machine. The stitches disappear into the seam, making a patch, block, border, or motif stand out from its background.

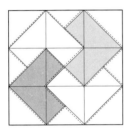

Single-Outline

Single-outline quilting is done parallel to and on one side of a seam (or the edge of an appliqué), ¼″ to ½″ away or far enough to clear the seam allowance. Quilting can be done closer to the seam (or appliqué edge) if done on the side of the shape without seam allowance.

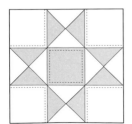
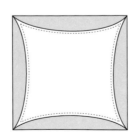

Double-Outline

Double-outline quilting is done parallel to and on both sides of a seam (or the edge of an appliqué), ¼″ to ½″ away or far enough to clear the seam allowance.

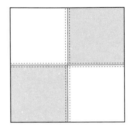

Echo

Echo quilting consists of multiple concentric outlines stitched either inside or outside a patchwork piece, appliqué, or quilted motif. The quilting lines are spaced evenly, ¼″ to ½″ apart (closer if stitched on the side without seam allowance) and can be expanded to completely fill the foreground or background if desired. (Optional: Stitch in-the-ditch before echoing either outward or inward.)

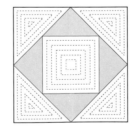

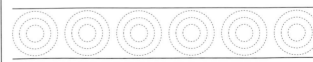

DIAGONAL

Diagonal quilting does not follow a motif outline but runs at an angle across part or all of a quilt. It may make use of the squareness of a block because a stitching line is easy to establish by marking from corner to corner, with additional lines parallel to the first if desired. Diagonal quilting can be used on isolated patches or blocks in the quilt center and/or on borders, and if

*well-planned and stitched over a large grid of squares, the
quilted lines can create attractive geometric designs.*

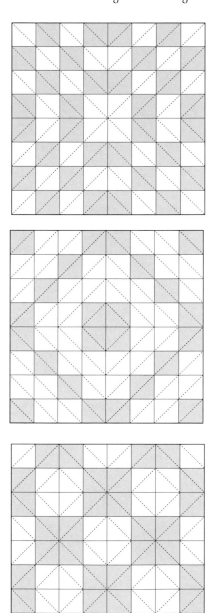

MOTIF QUILTING

Motif quilting is a showcase for stitched designs rather
than patchwork shapes. A motif is a design not necessari-
ly related to the shape of the fabric piece on which it is
stitched nor to any other part or aspect of the quilt top.
It can be large or small; simple or complex; straight-
edged or curved; single-outlined, double-outlined, or
echoed; and used just once or repeated.

   Many traditional motifs are available ready-made on
templates in a variety of sizes. Most motifs can be
enlarged, reduced, rearranged, or otherwise adapted for
any plain patch, block, or strip.

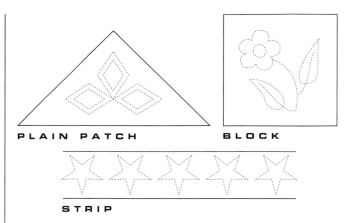

PLAIN PATCH   BLOCK

STRIP

Cables

Cable designs are made up of intertwined pairs of
regularly undulating lines. They come in all shapes, sizes,
and degrees of complexity.

Scrolls

Scrolls are another striking type of quilting design.
Curved or straight-edged, they can turn plain sashing or
borders into ornate frames.

Feathers

A feather design consists of a row of regularly spaced asymmetrical leaf or teardrop shapes along a single or double spine. The spine can be straight or undulating (good for strips or paralleling the outline of large patches) or it can form a shape (good for centering in blocks or large patches).

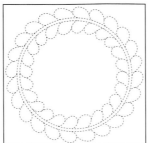

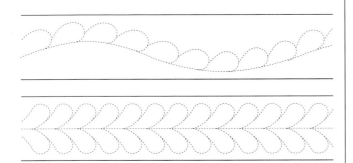

FILLERS, BACKGROUNDS, AND ALLOVER DESIGNS

Open interiors (such as inside a circle or heart) can be filled with a tessellation of squares, diamonds, triangles, clam shells, or other small, regular shapes. Backgrounds outside an appliqué or quilted motif can also be filled. The closely spaced lines of a filler tend to flatten the area over which they are stitched, creating a low-relief, textured appearance.

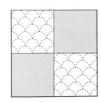
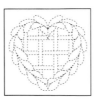

Stippling

Stippling is a type of quilting design that can be stitched by hand or by machine (called free-machine quilting; see pages 229–233, "Quilting and Tufting"). Stippling can take the form of straight rows of stitches regularly placed (lined up or staggered), random zigzags, or random curves. Stippled designs should always be closely spaced.

Allover Designs

Some designs, particularly geometrics, are stitched all over the quilt with no regard to the shapes or fabrics on the quilt top. Allover designs can be stitched from either the quilt top or the backing side.

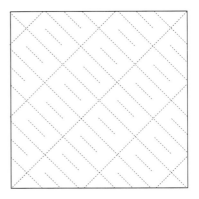

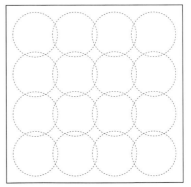

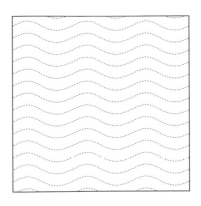

Quilting and Tufting

Quilted designs not only add visual interest to a project, but they also hold the quilt layers together. Tufting, or tying, is a less formal method of securing the layers, but it looks charming and is quick and easy to do.

QUILTING

Will you do your quilting by hand or by machine? If you hand-quilt, will you work with your project loose in your lap or stretched taut in a hoop or frame? How do you decide? You can begin by considering the following questions.

◆ *How much use and/or laundering is the quilt likely to get?* Machine-quilting is generally sturdier than hand-quilting.

◆ *Do you prefer the traditional look of hand-quilting or the modern look of machine-quilting?* Machine-stitches are continuous, even, and look as though they were made by machine. Hand-stitching creates broken lines, which have a softer look.

◆ *Do you prefer to stitch by hand or by machine?*

◆ *Are the quilting designs relatively simple and made of straight lines or gentle curves, or are they ornate and tightly curved?* Fancy curves are usually easier to stitch accurately by hand. Straight lines and gentle curves can be stitched more quickly, and just as accurately, by machine.

◆ *Will the quilting stitches be visible on the quilt top?* Stitches in-the-ditch won't show, and neither will most stitching done on allover print fabrics.

◆ *Is the time it will take to quilt your project a factor?* Machine-quilting is generally faster than hand-quilting.

◆ *Is portability of your quilting project a factor?* Individual blocks hand-quilted in a hoop are easily transported. A completely assembled project quilted by machine or in a frame is not.

◆ *How thick is your batting?* Thick batting is more difficult to machine-quilt than thin batting, and more difficult to transport.

Marking the Designs

Quilting designs are generally marked after piecing but before the quilt layers have been assembled and basted together (see also "Instead of Marking the Fabric," page 230). All marking (and pinning, basting, and quilting) should be done from the center of the quilt outward in all directions.

To prepare the quilt top, position it and the design (pattern, template, or stencil) right side up on the work surface, making sure the design is exactly where you want to stitch it on the fabric before taping, weighting down, or otherwise securing the design and the quilt top to prevent them from shifting during marking.

Reposition both the design and fabric as needed to mark the entire quilt top.

Mark the design with a fine-point nonpermanent marker, experimenting first on scrap fabric to be sure your marker will make thin, light lines that can be removed after quilting.

TRACING A PATTERN

If a source of illumination is placed behind a pattern and quilt top, the backlighting allows the design lines to show through to the front of the fabric for tracing. Prepare for tracing a quilting pattern as follows:

◆ **SUNNY WINDOW:**
Tape the pattern to a clean, dry window on a sunny day. Tape the quilt top over the pattern.

◆ **LIGHT BULB:**
Open a separating table and place a clean, dry sheet of glass over the opening. Place a lamp (minus the shade) on the floor below the glass, and turn it on. Tape the pattern to the top of the glass. Secure the quilt top over the pattern.

◆ **LIGHT BOX:**
Tape the pattern to the light box. Turn the light box on. Secure the quilt top over the pattern.

TEMPLATES AND STENCILS

Many templates and stencils can be purchased ready-made and adapted for almost any quilt by enlarging, reducing, extending, rotating, or flopping. To make your own template, see pages 217–218, "Preparing Patterns and Templates." To use a template, secure it on the quilt top with tape or weights and mark closely around the edges.

To make a stencil, mark the design lines on light-weight template plastic and cut along them with a double-bladed art knife, creating narrow slits connected by plastic bridges. To use the stencil, secure it on the quilt top and mark the design lines through the slits. Connect the marked lines on the fabric smoothly after removing the stencil.

PERFORATED PATTERNS

Mark the pattern on wrapping paper or other sturdy paper, then go over the design lines with a needle-pointed tracing wheel or with a sewing machine and an unthreaded needle.

To use the pattern, secure it on the quilt top and go over the perforations with chalk or stamping powder.

DRAFTING ON THE QUILT TOP

Individual straight lines and straight-edge shapes can be drafted directly on the right side of fabric with a marker and quilting ruler (and a protractor to measure angles that can't be verified with a ruler).

The lines forming the square grid on a cutting mat can also be used as a guide for drafting straight-line designs on small projects or individual blocks.

INSTEAD OF MARKING THE FABRIC

If you prefer not to put marks on your quilt top at all, you can use either of the following methods to make quilting guides after the quilt layers have been basted together.

◆ TEAR-AWAY PATTERNS:

Used for machine-stitched designs. Mark the pattern on tracing or tissue paper or on tear-away interfacing (one pattern for each time the design will be used). Baste the pattern on the quilt top, then quilt along the design lines through both paper and quilt. After quilting, tear away the paper pattern.

◆ TAPE:

Used for designs with straight lines. After the quilt layers have been assembled and basted, and the quilt is secured in a hoop or frame, apply an appropriately wide masking, drafting, or quilting tape to the quilt top as a guide for design lines that are parallel to seams and/or each other. Reposition the tape as needed until the quilting is complete, then remove it.

Assembling the Layers

Layer and baste the quilt on a large, flat work surface, such as a dining table, countertop, or floor. Having a helper for assembling and basting the quilt can make both processes faster and more enjoyable.

LAYERING

1. Place quilt backing wrong side up on work surface. If you are using a free-standing work surface, such as a table or island counter, which is smaller than the backing, center fabric on top so that equal lengths of fabric hang down on each side, like a tablecloth.

2. Position batting on top of backing, aligning edges. Baste batting and backing together with a single large cross-stitch in the center.

3. Center quilt top on batting, right side up.

BASTING

Hold the quilt layers together with straight pins, then baste with either thread or safety pins as follows:

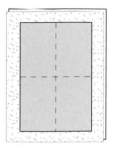

1. Baste along horizontal and vertical centers of quilt first, then diagonally in both directions.
- ◆ *For thread-basting: Make stitches about 2" long and 3" to 4" apart.*
- ◆ *For safety-pin basting: Space pins 3" to 4" apart.*

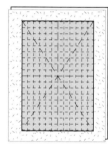

2. Make additional horizontal and vertical lines of basting 3" to 4" apart (or follow batting manufacturer's directions for spacing).
- ◆ *For quilting to be stitched in a hoop: Use thread for basting, and make stitches shorter (1" to 2" long) and more closely spaced (1" to 2" apart) because the hoop will be repeatedly moved and repositioned.*

Hand-Quilting

If you will be quilting in a frame, secure the long edges of the backing to the long parallel bars of the frame, following the frame manufacturer's directions, and rotate the frame bars during quilting to reach all areas of design.

If you will be working with the quilt in your lap (with or without a hoop), the edges should be temporarily finished, by basting the backing as self-binding (see pages 233-236, "Finishing the Quilt Edges"), to protect them during the quilting process. (Note: If you use a hoop, retighten and reposition it as needed to stitch all areas of design.)

Quilting stitches (running stitch or stab stitch) should be small (6 to 12 per inch), even, and equally spaced so they look the same on the back of the quilt as they do on the front.

Machine-Quilting

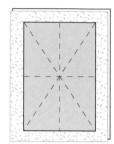

If you are machine-quilting a large project, the quilt should be rolled and folded before it is fed through the machine to make it easier to handle. It may be necessary to reroll and refold the quilt before each new area is stitched.

You can also place a table in front of the sewing machine to support the weight of the quilt as the machine moves it forward, instead of letting the quilt drop to the floor, which can create drag.

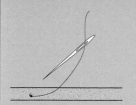

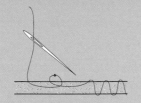

TO BEGIN A LENGTH OF THREAD:

Make a small knot in one end of the thread. Insert the needle into the quilt back and batting about 1" from where you want to make the first stitch and bring the needle out on the quilt top where the first stitch will be. Give the thread a tug to pull the knot up through the quilt back and embed it in the batting.

TO END A LENGTH OF THREAD:

Make a small knot in the thread a scant ¼" above the quilt back. Make a tiny backstitch and run the needle forward through the batting and bring it out on the quilt back about 1" away. Pull the thread taut and clip it, releasing the end to drop below the surface of the quilt back.

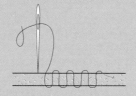

RUNNING STITCH
Only one thimble is required. Working from the top of the quilt, load the needle with as many stitches at one time as possible and pull the needle out with your upper hand.

STAB STITCH
Two thimbles are required. Working from both sides of the quilt, push the needle through the quilt with one hand and pull it out again with the other hand. Pull the thread completely through the quilt each time the needle exits the quilt.

Use a quilting foot or even-feed walking foot for machine-quilting. Adjust the stitch length for 6 to 12 stitches per inch, and loosen the upper tension if you use invisible thread. Just as for hand-quilting, machine-quilting should be done from the center of the quilt outward in all directions.

To begin and end a line of stitching, either make a few tiny backstitches and clip the threads close to the quilt top, or knot and embed long thread ends in the batting in the same manner as for finishing hand-quilting threads.

FREE-MACHINE QUILTING (STIPPLING)

To do stippling by machine, use a darning foot and either lower or cover the feed dogs. By eliminating the feeding action of the sewing machine, you have complete control over the movement of the quilt through the machine. There is no need to adjust the stitch length, because in addition to controlling the speed and direction of the stitches, your hands also determine the length of each stitch as they guide the quilt.

Insert the design area into a hoop for quilting, to keep it smooth and taut. Retighten and reposition the hoop as needed.

Trapunto

Trapunto is a type of quilting that is stuffed rather than padded, to create high-relief designs. A loosely woven lining such as muslin is stitched behind the quilt top with no batting between, then lengths of cotton cord or bits of loose fiberfill are used to stuff the stitched designs, working through the lining, to add dimension to the quilt top.

Fiberfill can be used for stuffing both large and small shapes. Cord-stuffing is more appropriate for small shapes. If the quilt top is a relatively sheer white or off-white fabric, using colored cord can add soft, subdued tints to the trapunto designs; this is also called shadow quilting.

After the stuffing and/or cording is completed, your project can then be layered and flat areas quilted with low-relief designs as usual.

PREPARING THE QUILT TOP AND LINING

1. *Mark trapunto (and traditional quilting) designs on quilt top.*
◆ **For stuffed designs, such as leaves or petals:** *Mark a single, closed outline for each shape to be stuffed.*

◆ **For corded designs, such as stems or outlines:** *Mark double outlines to form channels slightly wider than diameter of yarn to be used, maintaining a uniform distance between pairs of parallel lines.*

2. *Cut a muslin lining same size as quilt top.*
3. *Pin lining to wrong side of quilt top, aligning edges. Baste together as for traditional quilting but with 6" to 8" between columns and rows of basting stitches. Do not baste over trapunto designs. Machine-stitch ¼" from edges.*
4. *Quilt by hand or machine on trapunto design lines.*

STUFFING WITH FIBERFILL

1. Use appliqué scissors to carefully make a slit in lining at center of shape to be stuffed.

2. Working through slit, insert loose bits of fiberfill between quilt top and lining, using a blunt tool such as a stylus, crochet hook, or orange stick to distribute stuffing evenly.

3. Fill shape lightly but completely, checking front of quilt frequently. Do not overstuff.
4. Close slit with loose cross-stitches or whipstitches.

STUFFING WITH CORD

1. Working through lining, insert blunt rug or tapestry needle threaded with cord into one edge of shape to be filled, then bring it out at opposite edge.
2. Cut cord and trim ends to about ¼".

3. Insert additional lengths of cord until shape is entirely filled with side-by-side lengths of cord.

4. Use a blunt tool to distribute cord evenly across shape.
5. Trim cord ends close to the lining.

CORDING

1. Thread a long, blunt rug or tapestry needle with a 15" to 18" length of cord.
2. Working through lining only, use tip of needle to make a hole in channel large enough for needle to slip through.

3. Insert needle and slide it through channel between fabric layers as far as it can reach, then bring it out again on lining side. Pull cord until end disappears into needle entry point.

4. Reinsert needle at exit point and work it further along channel, then bring it up and re-enter channel as needed to cord its entire length.
◆ **At sharp corners:** Bring needle out at corner, then reinsert in same hole and run needle through adjacent leg of design, leaving a tiny loop of cord sticking out at corner.

5. To end a length of cord, bring needle out through lining and clip cord close to fabric, massaging the last needle exit point until end of cord disappears inside it.
6. When starting a new length of cord, overlap end of previous length at least ½" to be sure there are no gaps in corded outline.

TUFTING (TYING)

Tufting is the fastest way to quilt. It is appropriate for informal quilts, and if you want a fluffy, inviting comforter for your bed, tufting is the way to go.

◆ **BATTING:**
Use batting that is either bonded or needle-punched.
◆ **THREAD FOR TUFTING:**
Use one or more 36" lengths of crochet cotton, pearl cotton, buttonhole twist, or candlewick yarn and a large-eyed needle that is not so wide as to leave noticeable holes in the quilt.
◆ **WHERE TO TIE:**
You can tie on either the quilt top or backing side, depending on whether or not you want the knots and yarn ends to show when the quilt is displayed.

Tying can be done at strategic design points on the quilt top (corners or centers of blocks or strips, for example) or in an allover geometric design such as a square grid, disregarding the fabrics and seams, as long as the ties are spaced 4" to 6" apart. Tying can be charming on thin quilts, too. It's traditional for wool quilts and even crazy quilts.

How to Tie

1. Assemble and baste quilt layers in same manner as for quilting.

2. Make a single ¼"-long running stitch through all layers of quilt at the location to be tufted, leaving a 3" yarn end.

3. Make a single backstitch through the same holes formed by the running stitch; do not cut yarn.

4. Make another running stitch and backstitch at next and all subsequent locations to be tufted until length of yarn is used up.

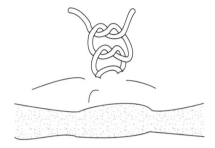

5. Clip halfway between adjacent stitches and trim ends if more than 3".
6. Tie each pair of yarn ends in a square knot.
7. Trim ends evenly to between ¼" and 1".

Finishing the Quilt Edges

*O*nce the layers of your work have been quilted or tied together, you will be ready to finish the edges. You may choose to turn the raw edges in toward the batting for a very clean finish, or use a simple binding, made either by wrapping the backing fabric onto the front or by applying a separate strip. If you are making a pillow, or want to give a large piece an important finish, you can add cording, prairie points, or ruffles before binding.

EDGINGS

Cording, prairie points, and ruffles are usually used as edgings for small items such as pillows, but you can use the following methods to apply them to a project of any size. If adding an edging to a quilt or wallhanging rather than a pillow, trim the backing, batting, and top edges even, then fold and baste the backing away from the seam allowance while applying the edging. Once the edging is attached, follow the directions for "Self-Binding with Edges Even" on page 235 to complete your piece.

Prairie Points

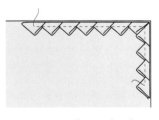

1. Press fabric squares in half diagonally twice, right side out (see individual project directions for size and amounts).

2. Pin triangles evenly along edges of project front with all double-folds facing the same direction. Lap adjacent edges, or slip single-folds inside double-folds. Stitch on seam line.

Cording

Cording is available ready-made in several sizes or can be made from your fabric. To make cording, encase a length of cord in a bias strip (see directions for making bias strips, later in this chapter) and stitch as close to the cord as possible, using a zipper foot.

Cording length = Perimeter of project + 1″

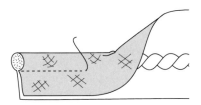

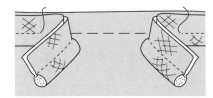

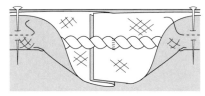

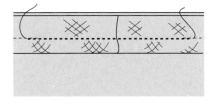

1. Pin cording around right side of work, beginning at center of one edge, so that stitching line of cord lies on seam line and flat/apron edge of cording is inside seam allowance.
2. Stitch to 1″ from cording ends: Pivot with needle in fabric at each corner. Clip flat/apron edge of cording up to seam line. Continue stitching next edge.
3. To finish cording ends, remove 1″ of stitching at each end of bias strip. Fold under ¼″ of fabric at one strip end; lap raw end over folded end. Trim cord so ends butt, and whip-stitch together. Refold bias strip; finish stitching.

Ruffles

For multiple ruffles, apply them one at a time as directed below, from narrowest to widest, one on top of the other, aligning seam lines.

Ruffle strip width = (Ruffle width x 2) + ½″
Ruffle strip length = (Perimeter of project x 2) + ½″

1. Stitch strip ends together to form a ring. Press seam open. Press ring in half lengthwise, right side out. Baste raw edges together.
◆ For straight-stitch gathering: Machine-baste along seam line and ¼″ away, inside seam allowance, leaving long thread ends.

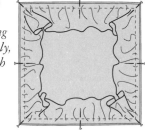

◆ For gathering over cord: Cut strong, thin cord (such as button thread) several inches longer than ruffle. Hold cord along seam line and machine-zigzag over but not into it, leaving equal cord ends free.
2. Flatten ruffle and fold in half twice, dividing it into eighths. Use pins to mark folds at basted edge of ruffle and to mark middle of each edge of front of work. Unfold ruffle and pin it in place, aligning markings on ruffle with markings and corners of project. Make sure seam allowances are aligned and pin heads face outward.
3. Pull up bobbin thread/cord, gathering ruffle to fit project. Adjust gathers evenly, allowing extra fullness at corners. Stitch along seam line.

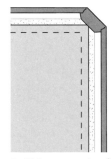

BINDING

Quilt edges can be self-finished or have a separate binding. Before binding, trim the quilt layers to size (see project directions).

Backing As Self-Binding

Baste the quilt layers together along the outer seam line. Place the quilt flat, right side up, and bind the quilt, making mitered or butted corners. (Note: Directions are given below for using the backing as the binding, but the quilt top can be used instead, if desired.)

Batting width beyond seam line = Binding width
Backing width beyond seam line = (Binding width x 2) + ½″

MITERED CORNERS

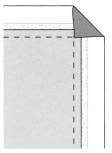

1. Press one corner of backing over quilt top, so that tip meets corner of seam line.

2. Trim away tip of corner. Press backing edges ¼″ to front.

3. Fold one edge over quilt top, covering seam line.

4. Fold adjoining edge, forming mitered corner. Slipstitch.

BUTTED CORNERS

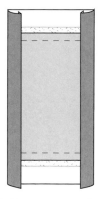

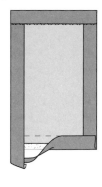

1. Press one pair of opposite backing edges ¼" to front. Fold backing to front again, covering seam line; pin.

2. Press and pin remaining backing edges in same manner. Slipstitch.

Self-Binding with Edges Even

Batting width beyond seam line = None (cut just outside seam line)

Backing width beyond seam line = ¼"

Quilt top width beyond seam line = ¼"

1. Press under ¼" on one opposite pair of quilt top edges and on corresponding backing edges. Press remaining quilt top and backing edges in same manner.

2. Pin together fabric folds, enclosing batting. Slipstitch folds together.

Separate Bindings

A separate binding can be one continuous strip or four individual strips, cut on the bias or the straight grain, plain or pieced, one layer of fabric or two. All pieced binding strips should be joined on a 45° angle to reduce the bulk once folded. Trim the quilt so that the edges of all three layers are even.

JOINING STRIP ENDS

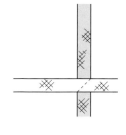

CUTTING BIAS STRIPS

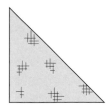

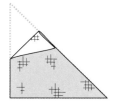

1. Cut a fabric square in half diagonally (along the bias).

2. Beginning at one 45° corner, fold fabric repeatedly, aligning bias edges.

3. Cut strips parallel to bias edge.
4. Join strip ends to make a longer strip.

SIMPLE CONTINUOUS BINDING

1. Press under seam allowance on one long edge and one end of binding strip.

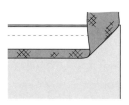

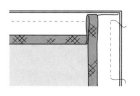

2. Pin and stitch binding strip to quilt top, aligning seam lines, beginning at center of one quilt edge with folded end of strip and stopping at seam line of next quilt edge; break threads.

3. To miter corner, press strip away from quilt on a 45° angle, then press it back over quilt. Stitch, beginning at end of previous stitching line (a tuck will form at corner). At beginning point, trim binding and lap ends 1"; stitch.

4. Fold binding over corners to backing, forming miters at tucks. Position long folded edge of binding over seam line, forming miters at corners. Slipstitch, stitching into miters to secure.

SCALLOPED EDGES

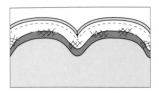

1. *Using bias strips, prepare simple or French fold binding as shown, opposite.*

2. *Stitch binding along seam line, beginning at center of one edge of quilt with folded end of strip, aligning seam lines. Ease around curves and clip seam allowance at inner points; lap and stitch ends.*

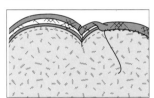

3. *Fold binding over quilt edges to backing; pin. Slipstitch, folding miters at inner points.*

INDIVIDUAL BINDING STRIPS

1. *Prepare simple binding.*

◆ ***For mitered corners:*** *Stitch binding strips to quilt top, making machine-stitched mitered corners (pages 207-211, "The Quilt Components"). Fold binding over quilt edges to backing; pin, making neat mitered or butted corners.*

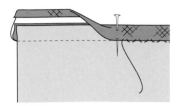

◆ ***For butted corners:*** *Stitch one pair of binding strips to opposite edges of quilt top. Trim ends even with quilt. Fold strips to backing; slipstitch. Apply second pair of strips to remaining quilt edges in same manner, folding ends under instead of trimming.*

Binding strip length = Length of quilt edge + 1″

FRENCH FOLD BINDING

French fold binding is made the same way as other separate, continuous bindings but uses more fabric because it is applied doubled.

Binding strip width = (Binding width x 4) + ½″
Binding strip length = Perimeter of quilt + 1″

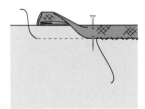

1. *Press under ¼″ at one end of binding strip. Press strip in half lengthwise, right side out.*

2. *Apply folded binding as for other bindings: Place raw edges of binding toward raw edge of quilt. It will not be necessary to press under free edge of binding as it is already folded.*

Preparing Your Quilt for Wall Hanging

You've finished your quilt! If it isn't going to be used on a bed, now is the time to consider how it will be displayed. Hanging on a wall, your quilt can be a dramatic focal point, but care must be taken to avoid the sags and tears that gravity may cause over time.

RINGS

Lightweight plastic rings (available in hardware stores) provide a simple way to hang a quilt. For a small wallhanging (up to about 20″ square), three ½″ diameter rings should be sufficient. For a larger project, buy enough rings so that they can be spaced 7″ to 9″ apart along the top edge of the quilt. You will need to affix one small nail (or picture hook) in the wall to support each plastic ring.

1. *Position one ring on backing, centered and 1″ below top edge. Sew center bottom of ring in place securely with a few hand-stitches, making*

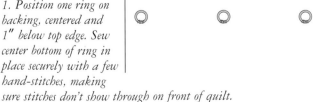

sure stitches don't show through on front of quilt.

2. Stitch a ring to each end of backing top, 1" from top and side edges.
3. Space any additional rings evenly between those already stitched in place.
4. To mount quilt, place rings over nails (or picture hooks) on wall.

SLEEVES AND HANGERS

A fabric sleeve can be sewn to the quilt backing for holding a wooden dowel or lattice strip that will support the weight of the quilt evenly and completely across the top. The larger and heavier the quilt, the sturdier the dowel or lattice strip must be. The ends of the dowel or lattice strip can extend beyond the quilt sides and be capped with decorative finials, or they can stop just short of the sides and support the quilt invisibly. Dowels can be supported with appropriate sizes of finishing (headless) nails, cup hooks, or small brackets. If using nails, be sure they extend sufficiently from the wall to hold the dowel.

Making a Sleeve

1. Cut a 3"-wide fabric strip 2½" shorter than width of quilt. (Note: If the quilt is very wide or heavy, make several shorter sleeves that will be spaced evenly across the quilt so the dowel can be affixed to supporting nails in several places.)
2. Press under ¼" on each edge of strip. Topstitch fold allowance at ends.
3. Center strip (sleeve) across quilt backing ½" below top edge; pin.
4. Hand-stitch long edges of sleeve securely to quilt backing, making sure stitches don't show through on front of quilt. Do not stitch ends.

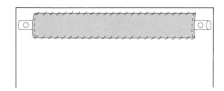

Invisible Hangers

1. Cut dowel (or lattice strip) 1" shorter than quilt width. If supporting with nails, drill a small hole ¼" in from each end.
2. Seal wood with polyurethane to prevent wood seepage from discoloring fabric.
Let dry thoroughly. (Note: Follow manufacturer's directions for method of application and drying time.)

♦ *If using nails to support quilt:* Measure, mark, and affix them to wall the same distance apart as holes in wood.
♦ *If using brackets or cup hooks to support quilt:* Measure, mark, and affix to wall appropriately.
3. Slide dowel (or lattice strip) through fabric sleeve, centering it between quilt sides so that holes in wood are at ends of sleeve.
4. To mount quilt, line up holes in fabric and wood with nails in wall. Press dowel in place, making sure nails go into holes.

Decorative Hangers

1. Cut dowel 1½" longer than quilt width. Seal wood with polyurethane and let dry.
2. Slide dowel through fabric sleeve, centering it so that equal amounts of wood extend at each side.
3. Attach finials to ends of dowel. (Note: Make sure at least one finial is removable so quilt can be taken down for cleaning.)
4. Measure, mark, and affix one sturdy nail, cup hook, or bracket to wall at proper distance for supporting ends of dowel.
5. To mount quilt, support exposed ends of dowel on nails or through cup hooks or brackets.

HOOK AND LOOP TAPE

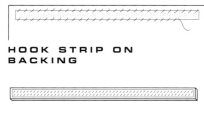

HOOK STRIP ON BACKING

LOOP STRIP ON LATTICE

Hook-and-loop tape (such as Velcro) provides another simple method for hanging a quilt and still allowing for it to be cleaned or laundered, because the tape is washable.

1. Cut a 2"-wide strip of hook-and-loop tape 2" shorter than quilt width.
2. Cut a 2"-wide wooden lattice strip same length as tape. Seal wood and let dry in same manner as for sleeves, above.
3. Separate the tape halves so that you have one strip with hooks (stiffer strip) and one with loops (softer strip).
4. Center the hook strip across quilt backing ½" below top edge. Hand-sew all strip edges securely in place, making sure stitches don't show through on front of quilt.
5. Attach the loop strip to lattice, aligning edges, using a staple gun or hot glue gun.
6. Measure, mark, and affix lattice securely to wall with nails, with loop strip facing out. Place nails ½" from lattice ends and in the center. Add nails between those already placed, dividing and subdividing spaces, using as many nails as needed to support weight of quilt.
7. To mount quilt, align hook and loop halves of tape. Press tape halves together firmly.

Caring for Quilts

Dampness and direct sunlight are the enemies of all textiles, so display or store your quilts away from both. With the proper care, a quilt can last for generations.

CLEANING

At some point all bed quilts and wallhangings need to be cleaned. Many quilters prefer using washable fabrics and batting so they won't have to subject their quilts to the harsh chemicals used by dry cleaners.

Fragile quilts can be vacuumed. Place a fine net or stocking over the vacuum foot to reduce suction. If the quilt is valuable, seek the advice of a professional before laundering or vacuuming.

Cotton and cotton-blend quilts can be washed as follows: Wash quilt in warm water with a small amount of mild detergent. By machine: Set washing machine on gentle cycle. Do not spin-dry. By hand: Use a large sink or tub. Do not wring dry.

Fold up quilt and carry it, wrapped in an absorbent towel or blanket, to where it will be dried. (Note: Never hang a wet quilt, because the weight of it can rip stitches and redistribute the batting unevenly.) Dry quilt flat (indoors on a floor, outdoors on the ground) on towels, a sheet, blanket, or mattress away from direct sunlight.

STORAGE

Quilts that aren't being used on a bed must be kept somewhere. They can be displayed on a wall (see pages 236-237, "Preparing Your Quilt for Wall Hanging") or on a quilting frame, or they can be folded and stored away.

Never store a quilt in plastic, which can cause discoloring or mildew. Instead, fold the quilt flat, pack it in acid-free paper, and store it in a bag made of cotton, such as a pillowcase. Periodically refold your quilt. Air it out at least once a year; choose a dry day and keep the quilt out of direct sunlight.

Appendix

USING THE CUTTING CHARTS

The sample cutting charts and schematics below demonstrate how these elements work together to provide the information needed to cut most of the pieces for any quilt project in this book. Any additional cuts, such as for binding, can be found in the Fabric and Cutting List for each project.

DRAFTING SCHEMATIC
Drafting schematics, which do not include seam allowance, are provided for your convenience as an aid in preparing templates.

DRAFTING SCHEMATIC
(No seam allowance added)

CUTTING SCHEMATIC
Cutting schematics, which do include seam allowance, can be used for preparing templates (with seam allowance included) but are given primarily as an aid for speed-cutting shapes using a rotary cutter and special rulers with angles marked on them.

CUTTING SCHEMATICS
(Seam allowance included)

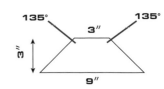

FABRIC AND YARDAGE
This column gives the color and amount of fabric needed to cut groups of shapes, rounded up to the next ¼ yard. To change the color scheme of a project, refer to the dimensions given for individual groups of shapes and use (combine them as needed) to calculate the new yardage.

FIRST CUT
Cut the number of pieces in the sizes indicated on either the lengthwise or crosswise grain unless otherwise stated, using templates or rotary cutting rulers. For 40"-long strips, cutting completely across the width of the fabric usually provides the most economical cuts.

SECOND CUT
Cut the number of pieces in the sizes and/or shapes indicated, referring to the cutting schematics for angles and cut sizes. Reversed pieces are designated by a subscript R (e.g., the reverse of a B patch is designated B_R) and can frequently be obtained from the same strips as their mirror images by cutting the two shapes alternately.

FIRST CUT			SECOND CUT	
Fabric and Yardage	Number of Pieces	Size	Number of Pieces	Shape
PLAIN PATCHES				
Red Solid ¼ yd.	1	3⅞" × 20"	8	A
	1	3½" × 40"	8	B
White Solid ¼ yd.	1	3⅞" × 20"	8	A
	1	3½" × 40"	6	C
SPEEDY TRIANGLE SQUARES				
Red Solid and White Solid ½ yd. each	2	16½" × 20⅝"	72	B/B[1]
BORDER				
Blue Check ½ yd.	2	2½" × 29"		
	2	2½" × 32"		

[1]See *Speedy Triangle Squares* (page 221). Mark 4 × 5 grids with 3⅞" squares.

BORDER
From ½ yd. blue check cut two 2½" × 29" and two 2½" × 32" border strips.

FOOTNOTE
Use the cited instructions for Speedy Triangle Squares and mark the grids in the layout indicated.

APPLIQUÉS
From ¼ yd. red floral cut 16 flowers and 8 buds. From ¼ yd. blue floral cut 56 leaves. Reversed pieces are designated by a subscript R and these patterns should be turned over before marking onto fabric.

APPLIQUÉS		
Fabric and Yardage	Number of Pieces	Shape
Red Floral ¼ yd.	16	Flower
	8	Bud
Blue Floral ¼ yd.	56	Leaf

8 RED SOLID A'S
From ¼ yd. red solid, cut one 3⅞" × 20" strip. From strip cut four 3⅞" squares. Cut squares in half to make 8 right-triangle A's.

6 WHITE SOLID C'S
From ¼ yd. white solid cut one 3½" × 40" strip. From strip cut six trapezoids.

FOOTNOTE REFERENCE
See the footnote underneath the chart for additional information about cutting this group of shapes.

Index